IN THE DEER WOODS

Books by Jerome B. Robinson

Hunt Close!
Training the Hunting Retriever
In the Turkey Woods
The Field & Stream Deer Hunting Handbook

IN THE DEER WOODS

Tips, Tactics and Adventure
Tales of Hunting for Whitetails,
Mulies, Moose, Elk, and Caribou

JEROME B. ROBINSON

THE LYONS PRESS

Printed in the United States of America

10 9 8 7 6 5 4 3 2 1

Library of Congress Cataloging-in-Publication Data is available on file.

CONTENTS

Acknowledgments vii

Introduction 1

1   On the Track of the King 5

2   Profile of a Tracker 13

3   Hunting Deer Near Water .23

4   Balancing the Deer Account 29

5   Canoe Hunt at Freeze-Up Time 37

6   Island of the Deer 47

7   Horseback Deer Hunt 57

8   How to Stillhunt 65

9   Hunting Migratory Whitetails 69

10   Deer Hunting as Good as It Gets 75

11   How to Have More Big Bucks 83

12   The Rewards of Rattling .87

13   Talk Like a Deer 101

14   Getting the Shot 107

15   Trophy Deer Management 117

16   My Most Memorable Buck 121

17   First Deer 127

18   Canoeing for Mule Deer 131

19   Guided by Lewis and Clark 139

20   Tobacco on the Water 147

21   Moosin' Around 153

22   A Word About Moose 161

23   Frank Rabbit—Legendary Hunter 165

24   Caribou House 173

25 The Power of Suggestion 185

26 Drive-In Caribou Hunting 187

27 Caribou—A Changing Challenge 197

28 Paddling to Rocky Mountain Elk 203

Index 209

ACKNOWLEDGMENTS

I am deeply indebted to the editors of *Sports Afield* and *Field & Stream* who, for more than 30 years, have been sending me off on hunting trips for stories printed in those magazines, some of which are republished here in somewhat longer form.

I also thank each of the people mentioned in these stories. They have all willingly passed along essential information, provided expert knowledge and experience, and shared in the disappointments and hard work as well as in the satisfactions that these hunting trips involved.

Finally, I thank Sherry, my wife, who has learned to accept that there are times when hunting comes before most everything else, and that those times happen every autumn.

INTRODUCTION

More than 30 years ago, when I was new to the outdoor writing business, I asked Lamar Underwood, who was then editor of *Sports Afield* magazine, what he really wanted me to do.

"Go out and live a life worth writing about," he replied.

That had to be the greatest assignment any writer was ever given. I took Lamar's instruction to mean that I was free to follow my interests, wherever they led, and to write about my experiences and photograph what I saw along the way. I've been doing just that ever since, for *Sports Afield* for more than 20 years and for *Field & Stream* the past 10 years.

Living a life worth writing about meant that hunting and fishing would not be just my hobbies; I had been invited to make hunting and fishing a way of life. It meant that I could pick up a camera and a gun or fishing rod and head for the woods or waters whenever I got the urge, even if the lawn needed mowing or the storm windows needed washing, because I would be *going to work*, and no one ever objects to that.

From my earliest memories I have been fascinated by hunting cultures. As a boy I read all I could about Native American hunters. I envied the hunter/gatherer way of life. I wished I could go live with the Indians, stalking deer and moose and caribou and elk, and paddling my canoe quietly into the unknown, living off the land.

Now I could do it and write about those experiences for a living.

Several of the stories included here came from hunting trips I've made with Native American people for whom hunting is a way of life. To them, hunting and the habits of animals are the only subjects worth a man's attention. They repeat hunting stories from generation to generation as a form of higher education. By telling hunting stories they pass along essential beliefs about the importance of having patience, of working hard to attain goals, and of respecting your quarry, as well as biological information about the habits of animals that influences how they should be hunted.

When you hunt with these people, you become absorbed in hunting. Everything you do is important to the hunt. At every moment you are either hunting or preparing to hunt. You eat and sleep in order to be strong for tomorrow's hunt. You travel to find where the hunting will be good. The weather is important only in so far as it affects what the animals will do.

All of us who hunt share genetic connections to a time when our ancestors hunted in order to live. I think it is important to nurture those connections, and I don't know any better way to do it than to plunge back into the hunting life from time to time, to camp out in the woods with a gun, some bare essentials, and a few good friends who share a need to connect with their hunter souls.

What follows is a collection of stories from hunting trips that taught me things about people, about Nature, and about myself, as well as information that hunters will find useful to know. I pass them along in the tradition of earlier hunters, with a devoted respect for the animals we hunt, and gratitude for all that the earth provides. —J.R.

1

ON THE
TRACK OF
THE KING

I first saw him the year I built my log cabin up in the big woods along the New Hampshire/Quebec border. I had gone down to the stream for a quick swim after finishing work and was sitting on the bank letting the breeze dry me when I looked up and there he was, a massive buck with high and heavy lyre-shaped antlers that stuck out past his ears and a pale gray face that was different from the face of any buck I'd ever seen. He was wading a riffle when he spotted me sitting there. For a moment our eyes met; then he was gone.

I remember noting that he had already rubbed the velvet from his antlers; they shone brightly in the red and golden light that was reflected in the water from the maples that were turning color on the ridge across from camp. I remember knowing the instant I saw him that he was the biggest buck I had ever seen. Even in that country, where many of the big ones weigh more than 300 pounds on the hoof, he was The King.

Next morning I went upstream to where he had crossed and studied the track where he had stepped in the hard clay at the water's edge. At the heel, his footprint was exactly as broad as my fist; the cloven hooves were longer than my middle finger. His dewclaws speared the ground a full three inches behind his heel. I let the look of the track sink in, and memorized its distinctive impression.

I didn't know it then, but that track was to become my talisman. Over the years it would lead me to places I might never have visited unless the track had taken me there. For a decade now I have searched for that particular track on each November snow; when I have found it, I have followed it—through cedar swamps on the back sides of mountains I would never have crossed, to hardwood ridges with long views into Canada that I would not likely have witnessed otherwise. The tracks once led me to a spectacular waterfall in the most remote headwaters of a river I fish for trout; since then I have hiked back there in the summer and caught colorful 10-inch brookies from the deep green pool below the cascade.

Following the track of The King has shown me the hidden places where deer yard up in winter, and where they can be expected to begin gathering after the first deep snow. It has revealed ancient migration routes that deer follow from many miles away to reach these special yarding areas. The King's track has taught me where there are mountaintop thickets in which a deer can stand and let a man walk past at close range and not be seen, and taken me to countless places where deer go to feed on beechnuts, paw for fern roots, nibble mushrooms, rub their antlers, make scrapes, and do their rutting. By following the track of The King, I have learned the country I hunt.

How I know it is the same buck's track that I am following year after year, and not some other big one's, is difficult to explain. I can only tell you that I *do* know. I know it just as you know your own track when you see it in the snow, even though other hunters wear similar boots and leave similar signs. Their tracks are similar, but they are not yours, and you know it.

He travels over identical routes to the exact places he has taken me to before. He uses the same rubs year after year and returns to beds I remember him using at other times. When I'm trailing him and he knows it, he has foiled me with the same tricks that have gotten rid of me on earlier occasions. But mostly I know his track because the sight of it strikes some mystical chord in some rarely visited attic of my hunter's soul, one that stridently proclaims, "That's him!"

And, just often enough to prove there's no mistake, I have seen The King himself making the tracks.

I have only had him in my sights twice. The first time was the same year I saw him standing in the stream.

I was halfway up on the ridge across from camp on a frosty popcorn morning when the frozen leaves made quiet walking impossible. I had paused to lean against a tree and watch when I heard a deer up above me.

There was no mistaking the sounds. He would take a few quick steps, then stop. A few more quick ones, then stop again. I turned slowly and brought the rifle around to where it would jump to my shoulder smoothly when the deer appeared. Suddenly the buck was coming.

He was running now, taking the broken ground in long bounds that ended in mighty crashes, coming downhill right at me. When he broke into view there was no mistaking him for another deer. The high and heavy lyre-shaped rack, the pale gray face, and the massive brown body with legs as thick as those of a Jersey heifer were recognizable features of the buck I knew.

My rifle rose to my shoulder as he came tearing past about 40 yards away, and when I fired the scope was filled with hair and the crosshairs were riding the back edge of his shoulder. I lowered the gun, sure that I had hit him right behind the shoulder and that he was running dead on his feet.

Only after he had disappeared and I had followed his tracks for several hundred yards without finding first the blood and next the piled-up carcass that I expected, did I return to the spot from which I'd fired and recreate the scene. I left my hat where I had stood and walked straight out to where the deer had been, then turned around and faced where I had shot from. Then I saw the bright fractured splash on the side of a maple sapling 10 feet away that my bullet had pierced instead of the deer.

The next year The King made another mistake and I had him dead to rights, but he bamboozled me.

I was driving my pickup over the mountain we call Buck Hill when I saw him bedded out in the middle of a clear cut. Right out in the open, plain as day, his big rack sticking up and shining in the sun, his rut-swollen neck as thick as a tree trunk. I gawked, but kept on truckin' without changing the engine's rpms until I got over a rise and out of sight.

Then I braked the truck, left the engine running so that there would be no vibratory change to arouse his suspicions, and slipped my rifle off the rack. As I crept into the woods, I slid a single round into the chamber. I closed the bolt quietly, then moved through a spruce thicket to the edge of the clear cut.

He was still there, not a hundred yards away, lying down with only his head and neck showing. There was no wind. The sun was in his eyes. I eased to the side of a solid tree and leaned against it as I raised my rifle. He saw no motion and remained perfectly still. In fact, it seemed to me he was too still.

I studied him through the scope. His antlers were surely like those I remembered, but something about him seemed too perfect. His eyes were shining in the sunlight, his black nose glared in the sun as if it were varnished. His sleek brown neck with every hair in place looked groomed, his white throat patch bleached. He held one ear out straight and the other slightly dipped. I'd seen that pose on taxidermy mounts a hundred times.

FAKE! My brain shouted the word. FAKE!

A warden's counterfeit deer way out here in the woods? It didn't make sense. What could I be doing wrong? I was well off the road and, anyway, the road was only a temporary seasonal logging track. How could this be a trap? My brain reeled with doubts and paranoia, but my finger stayed off the trigger as I continued to study the big deer's immobile head.

"I don't know why I'm not allowed to shoot here, but that is definitely a stuffed deer head propped up out there, and I'm not falling into the trap," I told myself, lowering the rifle.

Then, far off in the valley, a log truck geared down for a hill and, at the sound, the big deer turned his head.

"You paranoid fool, that's your deer!" my inner voice chuckled.

Now I re-raised my rifle, re-took my lean, brought the crosshairs up onto the too-bleached throat patch on the too-groomed neck, but by then I was shaking, and when I squeezed off the shot I felt the flinch and knew the bullet was going high and to the outside.

The buck and a doe that had been lying unseen behind him now jumped to their feet but, hearing the shot as an echo, they both faced the hardwood forest behind them and stood staring with their backs to me. I dipped in my pocket for another shell and hurriedly tried to reload, but in my haste, I failed to pull the bolt back all the way and eject the spent shell. When I crammed the new one in and slammed the bolt shut again, I solidly jammed both brass cartridges in the breech.

My eyes remained on the buck while my hands fidgeted to free the jam and get a live round in place. Hearing my jittery, rattling sounds, The King now turned his head and faced me. Then the doe started bounding away, and a moment later he switched his tail and left, too, leaving me to cuss myself and question what ever made me mistake the biggest buck I've ever had in my sights for a taxidermy mount.

Later that same year I saw him once more. I had picked up his tracks on a wet, snowy morning and followed them into a copse of thick spruce and fir just above the stream. I was moving silently in the snow, traveling into the wind just as he had done, and knowing by the freshness of his tracks that he was only minutes ahead. I was moving in suspended animation, ready to see him at any moment.

Suddenly he was there, not 30 yards away, looking right at me, his breath steaming around him, his big rack wet and brown and crusted with snow. I raised my rifle as his head began to turn away, shouldered it as his hind legs compressed, and brought the gun to bear just as he began his leap, but then the picture went blank. My scope was plugged with snow. I couldn't see him at all.

Judging by his immense size and the thickness of his antlers, The King must have been at least 4 years old back then, which means he must be 14 now. As the years pass he has become increasingly crafty and nocturnal. When I see him at all these days, it is only at long range and only for a moment.

Several times he has lost me by running straight to the top of the ridge across from camp where there is a big, thick patch of hardwood saplings. You can't move in that patch without bumping against saplings and making them shake and rattle in their top branches. The growth is so thick you can't see more than a few yards at eye level.

He goes in there, and his tracks show that he immediately lies down. If I begin to get close to him, he stands up and flits through the saplings for 40 or 50 yards, then lies down again. He'll do this for hours, never leaving the sapling patch, just moving around me and bedding down again.

I figured out what he was up to once when the snow was deep. Wherever he bedded in the snow I found the long impression of his throat where he had extended his neck and rested his chin in the snow. When I got down in the snow myself and put my chin at snow level, the whole thing became clear. Bedded, with his head held low, he could see my feet moving among the bases of the saplings long before he could have seen my body if he had been standing up trying to see me at a level where branches obscured his view.

I know the locations of dozens of scrapes he uses every year, each one overhung by a branch that he nuzzles and licks and marks with his scent. But he patrols his scrapes only at night and never goes near them in daylight.

For years now he has been moving mostly at night, leaving tracks that are hours old when I find them in the morning. By daylight he is up on the ridge or over on the back side of one of the mountains that stretch away toward Canada. And yet, several times each week he still crosses at the riffle just above my camp, where I first saw him many years ago, and I can pick up his trail in the morning within rifle shot of my doorstep.

He has never been the kind of deer that goes bounding around the woods when he knows he's being followed. Instead, he moves only a short distance and then stops in thick cover watching, listening, and taking scents from the air.

Six times in the 10 years I have tracked him, The King has ended my hunt and thrown me off his trail for one more year by leading me to another buck that I have shot instead. I don't mean that I mistook another deer for The King. No, each time it's happened I simply came upon another pretty good buck and decided, "This one's good enough for this year."

At first I thought it was just coincidence that I would find another buck standing in The King's tracks, but then I started wondering if I would have ever seen the deer I've shot if The King had not led me to them. To shoot a deer, you and the deer must come to the same place at the same time. The only reason I was in position to make those kills was that The King had led me there. I now believe that The King has learned to save himself by sacrificing his lieutenants.

Each year I think I know his habits well enough to predict where he is likeliest to go when followed. I suppose that's the way to get him—put another man on his track while I try to predict what he'll do and attempt to intercept him, but at heart I am a solitary hunter and am not drawn to group efforts.

I didn't hunt him much last season. I can't explain why. I told myself I was waiting for deep snow that never came, but I know that was not the whole reason.

On the last night of deer season I had a dream. I had followed him way out toward Canada to a little set of knobby spruce-topped hills where he has often given me the slip. Suddenly he rose up from his bed and stood before me. In my dream I could feel my thumb nudge the safety off as the rifle came up. I saw the crosshairs settle behind his shoulder and felt my finger begin to tighten on the trigger. Then I hesitated for one last look at him.

I awoke startled.

Outside it was snowing hard and deepening fast. But deer season was over.

I sometimes think I know just where he would have been bedded under the thickening blanket of snow that morning but, of course, I can't be sure.

2

PROFILE
OF A
TRACKER

Country wisdom says that if you put a boy on a stump and tell him to stay there until a buck comes along, and one does come along and he shoots it, he will be a patient stump-sitter all his life.

But if the boy gets bored and leaves the stump to have a look around, and subsequently shoots his first buck while he is sneaking through the woods, you have the makings of a stillhunter: a tracker who hunts for deer rather than relying on the deer to come to him.

My New Hampshire neighbor and frequent hunting partner, Alfred Balch, was never a patient stump-sitter.

"I get curious about what's happening over the hills," he admits. "I figure you are only going to see deer if you or the deer are moving. One of us has to move or there's not going to be an encounter."

Alfred was taught about the ways of wild things by his father back when it was expected that a man would teach his son to hunt. He shot his first buck when he was 10.

"Dad was following a fresh track up on Bear Hill and I was tagging along behind him," Alfred recalls.

"Suddenly Dad stopped and whispered, 'Do you see him?'

"I couldn't see the deer, so Dad lifted me up on a stump. I could see it then. Dad handed me his rifle and whispered, 'Shoot him like I showed you how.'

"I aimed that big gun and let roar and the deer went down. I dropped the rifle in the snow and ran to the deer. It was dead. A 6-pointer. When Dad came up I said, 'Isn't he a beauty?'

" 'He's a beauty a'right,' Dad said. 'But next time don't throw my rifle in the snow.' "

For five more years, until he was old enough to draw a hunting license and hunt alone, Alfred shared his father's rifle and got a deer each year.

"We always got our deer by going out and looking for them," Alfred recalls. "Dad taught me that if you want to learn about deer, you've got to track them. See where they're feeding, what they're eating; find out where they bed in different kinds of weather and at different times of year."

Forty years later, Alfred still goes out tracking deer the year around, roaming the nearby mountains whenever he gets a chance, gathering knowledge about the deer so that when he goes out to hunt, with a bow in September, a muzzleloader in October, or a high-powered rifle in November, he knows where a particular buck is most likely to be.

"A deer track always leads to more deer tracks," Alfred says. "Following tracks teaches you the patterns deer follow. Tracking teaches you about their habits. You won't learn those things sitting on a stand.

"Tracking gets you in shape, too," he adds. "You hitch onto the track of a rutting buck and you're going to cover some country. If you do a lot of tracking you get conditioned to moving in the woods and balancing yourself so you're not so awkward and noisy."

Hunting with Alfred, I am often struck by the way he moves, for I rarely see him move at all. I see him stopped beside a tree someplace, and later I see him stopped beside another tree, but I seldom see him in motion.

When I mentioned the mystery of how he gets from place to place, he said, "Walk for one minute, stop for three."

But I think he meant that he stops three times as much as he walks, for if he really moved for a minute at a time, I'd see him more than I do, and so would the deer.

He stops and studies the woods around him for a long, long time. He looks for a piece of a deer, not a whole deer. The crooked line of a deer's hind leg sticking out from behind a tree, the straight line of a deer's back: these are the kinds of pieces he searches for. "I know I'm going to see a moving deer—it's the one that is standing still or bedded that I'm looking for," he says.

Before he moves, Alfred plans his next few steps so that he can take them without looking down at the ground.

"Know where you're going to step before you start walking so that you don't have to look at the ground when you're moving," he told me once. "Keep your eyes open and watch for deer, not your feet. If you have to look at your feet, you're moving too fast.

"If you're seeing deer's flags, that's another indication that you're moving too fast," he adds. "Those are deer that saw you first. You can't go too slow."

Alfred's way of hunting is to find a good track and work it. Before the snow comes, when tracks sometimes appear to be nothing more than obscure disturbances in the frozen leaves, he reads them with his fingers.

"Press your two fingers right down into this track, right to the bottom," he commands. "Feel it?"

When you do it, the track becomes alive to your touch. A mere hole in the leaves until you touched it, the track now takes form. You can feel the length and breadth of the long cloven hoof, can feel whether the points on the bottom of the track are sharp or rounded.

"Now pull the leaves out of that track and you can see it," Alfred adds.

I once told Alfred about a study I had read in which biologists had measured the hooves of 2,500 deer and determined it is impossible to tell the sex of a deer by its tracks alone.

"That's because they measured the feet on dead deer," Alfred shot right back. "It's not just how big a track is that tells you if it was made by a buck or doe, it's the way they put their weight on their feet.

"In the fall when a buck's neck is swollen, a buck carries his weight on his heels," he explained. "That tends to make his toes spread apart when he is walking and brings his dewclaws in contact with the ground more often. A doe generally holds her toes together when she's walking and makes more of a heart-shaped track. Her dewclaws only show when she's moving fast.

"In shallow snow a buck drags his toes so it's plain to see even if the snow is only an inch deep. Does pick their feet up and set them down clean," Alfred continued.

"Where the tracks go tells you something, too," he added. "A buck in the rut will generally be moving alone, striding right out through the woods, not on any particular trail, really covering the country.

"Droppings tell you some more," Alfred said. "A buck dribbles his droppings as he moves along. A doe tends to drop them in a clump.

"A buck's track will lead to his scrapes, hooking around bushes and trees he has rubbed. You put all these factors together and you know damn well when you're on a buck track."

Why do bucks put their weight on their heels?

"Just look at a buck in fall," Alfred says. "His neck is swollen up twice its normal size and, as the rut wears on, he loses weight on his back and loins. He's carrying most of his weight up front, so he balances it by setting back on his feet."

Alfred locates big buck tracks by hiking a wide route around the edge of country where he expects deer to be moving, looking for the freshest signs of an extra big one.

Before taking a track and following, he often makes a swing around the outside of the country the track leads into, to see if it comes out the other side.

"No use following a track into a place when you can check to see if the deer stopped in there or moved through," he says. "Of course, lots of times you can't check the far side, so then you have no choice, you have to follow the track from where you found it."

Identifying the freshness of a track depends on accurate observation of weather conditions. "You have to pay attention to when things happen to know when a track was made," Alfred explains. "For example, if you know it stopped raining at 3 o'clock and you find a track that hasn't been rained on, you know it was made after 3 o'clock. It helps to remember what time frost came and what time the ground thawed and when snow started or stopped. These things tell you how fresh a track is."

When there is no snow on the ground deer tracks in leaves are more noticeable if you look ahead, rather than looking down at them. The tracks show up as a visible line of disturbance. When the line of tracks is obscure, getting your eye down close to the ground makes them show up distinctly.

"Crouch down and squint out there along the ground," Alfred told me one day when we were hunting on loose, newly fallen leaves. "See that line of tracks? Now stand up. You can hardly see them at all."

When you encounter a bunch of similar deer tracks going both into and out of a certain section of woods, it can be difficult to know which way the deer went last. "The best bet is to go in the direction that most of the tracks go," Alfred advises. "If a deer goes into a piece of woods and then comes back out and finally goes back in again, most of the tracks will be headed in the direction the deer went last."

Tracks tell you a lot about the deer and show you where they have been, but you have to rely on your wits to figure out where they are going.

When Alfred works a track, he doesn't just walk along following it. He'll follow the track a bit to get a sense of where it is going, then he swings out on the downwind side and hunts on a course that is parallel to the track. Every so often he loops back to the track to keep alert to its general direction.

When a buck stops to rest, he will often turn and walk straight downwind for 50 to 100 yards, then travel back parallel to its track for a little way before bedding down below the top of a rise of ground. This puts the deer in a position to overlook its backtrack so it can see, smell, and hear anything that may be following.

"By hunting parallel to a track on the downwind side, you have a chance of coming up on the buck without being seen or scented," Alfred explains.

When he hunts with a partner, Alfred likes to have one man follow the track while the other moves parallel on the downwind side as far out as he can be and still keep the track-follower in sight.

"That's a deadly method," he declares. "It's how Dad and I always hunted. It requires two people who hunt at the same slow pace, can move quietly, and have sharp eyes. By keeping an eye on the tracker, the wing man knows he's staying in line with the track."

Moving quietly takes practice and requires learning a different way of shifting your weight.

"Hold your weight back on the foot that's under you while you place your front foot and then roll your weight forward," Alfred instructed me one day when the leaves were frozen and it sounded as if I were walking on corn flakes. "If you feel a twig or something that is going to make noise under your foot, shift your weight back to your rear foot while you make a correction. Move slowly and don't just fall forward onto your front foot."

No one can move in complete silence, even in the best of conditions, but there are a few things you can do to limit the noise you make.

"The loudest sounds are those you make above the ground," Alfred notes. "The snap of a branch that catches on your coat carries farther than the crunch of a twig beneath your foot. Dry stubs that stick up from logs are particularly noisy—catch your foot on one of them and it makes a snap like a rifle shot.

"You're always going to make some noise, but you can try to make noises that sound like a moving deer rather than a man," Alfred instructs. "A deer takes a few steps and then stops for a long period—men tend to clump along with steady footfalls that warn wildlife from long distance."

Alfred moves in the shadows, avoiding open places as much as possible. He stops beside a tree and waits in the shadow of that tree, studying what's ahead until he is ready to move to the shadow of another tree.

"Stopping beside a tree breaks up your silhouette, and it also gives you something solid to lean on if you need to take a long shot," he reasons. "Staying in the shadows is just common sense; it makes you harder to see."

The sight of any deer stops Alfred in his tracks. "Whenever you have a deer in view, stop and watch," he advises. "A doe is often followed by a buck that may be moving 10 or even 15 minutes behind her. Her attitude will often tell you if there are other deer around. If she stares in one direction frequently, chances are good another deer is there."

Being alert to sounds is another important aspect of stillhunting.

A few years ago I was hunting caribou with Pat Cleary, a Montagnais Indian from central Quebec who was a fine tracker. Pat had been making slow but sure progress in following a single caribou bull across a long expanse of broken granite when he suddenly raised his head and listened.

Canada geese were clamoring in the distance.

"Those geese see the caribou," Pat said. "C'mon, we'll go over there."

We trotted for nearly a mile to a little lake surrounded by low willows. A big flock of geese sat on the water, still talking. Near them, on the wet, sandy shore, was the fresh track of the caribou bull we were after.

"We just gained a couple of hours on him," Pat said with satisfaction. An hour later we caught up with the bull; his double-shoveled rack now hangs in my cabin.

Sounds made by birds and squirrels can often tip you off to movement in the forest. When blue jays call excitedly or red squirrels begin to chatter, ask yourself what they could be talking about. Such sounds are often worth investigating.

For the past three years, Alfred has been carrying a thin stick in his pocket. It is exactly the width of the biggest walking buck track Alfred has seen passing through his hunting territory in recent years. Whenever he comes across a large track, Alfred pulls the stick out of his pocket and checks to see if it was made by The Big Guy.

One day Alfred took me high up on a hardwood ridge to show me The Big Guy's track.

"When he's in this country, this is one of the places he travels," Alfred said.

"A big buck has his own runways that are separate from the more noticeable trails the other deer travel," he continued. "When you are tracking a big buck it's important to remember exactly where it comes from and where it goes." Gradually, Alfred has put together a mental map of The Big Guy's travel pattern.

"One of these days we're both going to come to the same place at the same time," he declares. "Then it'll be up to me to see him before he sees me."

Each year Alfred is restless until he finds The Big Guy's track after hunting season has ended. Last year he didn't find the track he wanted until long after Christmas, and he worried that The Big Guy had died. Then one bright January day he stopped me on the road. He reached in his pocket and pulled out his measuring stick and held it up to me.

"He's still up there," he said. "I found his track crossing the ridge this morning."

3

HUNTING DEER NEAR WATER

When most deer hunters take to the hills, I go the other way and head for water. The reason is self-explanatory: Most deer hunters will not be there. In fact, so few hunters use boats to gain access to good deer hunting country that I can be pretty well assured of having a big piece of country to myself whenever I use a boat.

There is another reason, too. The edges of waterways are natural game corridors, and deer spend a lot of time in the narrow belts of cover that typically parallel the edges of rivers, lakes, and streams.

There is a heavily used game trail just a few yards back in the woods from every waterway in remote country. You can count on it. I know from doing a fair amount of canoe-camping, that a trail will always be there for me to use for portaging around major rapids or waterfalls. That tells me something about where deer travel.

The edges of waterways are natural boundaries to deer territories. Unless a deer makes up its mind to cross water, it is going to turn left or right and follow a shoreline game trail whenever it comes to a major waterway.

Because of the additional sunlight that strikes the open edges of the forest in shoreline locations, a variety of shrubs, grasses, and herbaceous foliage is available near waterways that is not available in the darker regions of the forest, making the shoreline belt particularly attractive to does with growing offspring. And, of course, when the breeding season occurs, bucks that are moving according to their natural habits are drawn to the areas most frequented by females.

Don't construe this to mean that I hunt from my boat, expecting to encounter a deer along the bank. I do not. I use the boat simply as a conveyance to reach deer country that is less accessible from the road; then I go ashore and hunt on foot.

Nor do I mean that I hunt only in the shoreline corridor, though I do put in a lot of time there. Once ashore, I follow the sign and let it show me where the deer are spending most of their time. If the shoreline trail shows extra-heavy use and leads from one heavily used feeding area to another, then I may hunt the belt of cover that parallels the waterway. But if the sign shows that deer are moving to the shoreline from somewhere else and merely passing through, then I follow the sign to see where it leads. Such sign usually takes me to an area where deer are concentrating for some obvious reason such as a heavy acorn crop on a nearby oak ridge or a logging job where nutritious hardwood tops have been dropped to the ground.

The thing I can be relatively sure of when reaching a hunting territory from the water side is that the deer will be following their natural habits rather than being pushed around by the presence of too many hunters in the woods. This gives me the opportunity to study the sign and try to determine where I am most likely to encounter a buck as he carries out his regular pattern of movement.

This advantage is not a guarantee of success, to be sure, but it pits me against a quarry that is more predictable than a frightened one that is mostly motivated to run and hide.

I realize that many hunters prefer to hunt in the vicinity of other hunters for the very reason that human presence keeps deer moving. I'm just not drawn to that kind of hunting. I'd rather be alone in good deer country, counting on my ability to observe tracks and other sign that tell me where deer are feeding and bedding and how they move from one site to another. Then it becomes a contest between me and the deer, with the advantages stacked heavily in the deer's favor.

Long ago an old Maine hunter told me that "a buck likes to bed where he can listen to running water." That seemed pretty far-fetched when I first heard it, but afterwards I began noticing a little more about where bucks choose to bed, and I was surprised to find how many times the old-timer's advice proved correct. Now, when I come to a place where I can hear a bubbling little woodland brook or the sounds of waves lapping a shoreline, I look around for the nearest piece of high ground that offers cover and check it out. You'd be amazed how often there is a well-used buck bed in exactly that type of location. When I find one, I file that spot away as a likely place to find a buck someday when conditions are right.

Knowing spots like this helps me plan my hunting pattern. When the wind is in my favor, I'll return to these bedding places, slipping in from the uphill side, then sitting quietly and watching. Twice I have killed good bucks that were bedded unseen when I crept in, but which later stood up and moved, offering a shot from where I sat hidden. On several other occasions I have killed bucks that were returning to these regular bedding places after I had already taken a stand overlooking them.

"The sound of running water is like music to a buck," the old-timer had declared. I don't know about that, but I can vouch for the fact that bucks frequently bed within the sound of running water.

Wherever deer territories overlap, whitetails interact with one another to a larger degree. That is why shoreline trails often show an inordinate amount of buck sign in the form of rubs and scrapes. Many bucks travel them. Bucks get extra-competetive when they are in places that other bucks visit frequently and demonstrate their vigor and readiness by repeatedly leaving their marks.

When I find a place where several saplings are rubbed and ground scrapes appear close together, I know that I am in a location where bucks expect to encounter each other and that they will be alert to the sounds of a competitor's presence. That tells me I am in a particularly good place to use a grunt call or rattling antlers, and I begin scouting around for a hiding place from which I can make the sounds of a pair of bucks fighting or of a single buck that is looking for a fight.

When you are hunting in an area where deer are moving naturally and not being run around by other hunters, you can learn a great deal by studying the tracks—not just how big they are and where they go, but also when they were made. This requires paying attention to when things occur during the day and night. Notice what time it is when a thaw begins and the time when mud and snow freeze hard. What time did rain or snow begin falling, and when did it stop? Knowing when these events happened helps you identify what time a track was made, and with that knowledge you can begin to learn about the daily movement patterns the deer are following. And once you understand this, you can often predict where they will be.

When you locate the track of a large deer, follow it and see where it leads. By combining this information with some idea of when the tracks were made, you can begin to narrow down the probabilities of where and when you and that deer are likely to come to the same place at the same time.

Then, it's up to you to see him before he sees you.

Whenever I travel to hunt deer in an area where the terrain is unknown to me, I first check the map for waterways that would give me access to a section that would be hard to reach from the road. I can be pretty sure that the hunting pressure there will be minimal or nonexistent.

Over the years I have used waterways to lead me to hunting sites in states I have never hunted before, and the results have always been rewarding. My hunting partners and I have used canoes to reach hidden deer hunting hotspots in Montana, Wisconsin, Quebec, Maine, Minnesota, Ontario, New Hampshire, and Vermont, and we have always found that using boats gives you access to country where others are unlikely to be hunting, and where the deer are likely to be acting naturally. Hunting them successfully then depends more on skill and less on luck.

As the hunting season progresses, bigger bucks often move out of country where the hunting pressure is heavy to seek quieter haunts. They draw back from the areas close to roads and head for the places where hunters are less likely to be.

A boat gives you the same opportunity.

And you know what else? It's usually a lot easier dragging a deer down to the riverbank and taking it home in a boat than dragging it out to a road.

4

BALANCING THE DEER ACCOUNT

I come from a family of great dreamers. My grandfather had dreams that were so real to him that he once called the police to report burglars in the dining room stealing the silver. He waited for the law to arrive sitting at the top of the stairs with a loaded .32 caliber Iver Johnson revolver, and when the policemen showed up, Gramp tucked the pistol into his bathrobe pocket and made them coffee while they checked the house. Nothing was missing, and there was no sign of forced entry.

"Huh," Gramp snorted. "Must have been one of my dreams."

Another time he was ready to sue an appliance manufacturer he said had stolen a slogan he wrote for an advertising contest. He said the company was using the slogan on television and had never paid him for his winning entry. Of course, there had never been a contest. It was another of Gramp's dreams.

I have very realistic dreams myself. When I go to sleep at night it is often like going to the movies. It is never surprising to me when problems I encounter during the day are dealt with and sometimes solved in my dreams at night.

This time it happened when we were camped on a river in northwestern Wisconsin hunting deer. After two days of tramping through woods with deer sign so thick it looked like a sheep pasture, none of us had seen a buck—not even a tail that might have been attached to a buck. All the sign indicated that the deer, recognizing the danger of moving during daylight, had become totally nocturnal. We were getting royally skunked, and it was clear we needed some help.

I worried that perhaps I had jinxed this hunt.

You see, just a week before going to Wisconsin, I had killed a big 8-point buck back home in New Hampshire. You know how you tend to say a word of thanks when for no explainable reason some mysterious force puts you and a big buck in the same place at the same time? Well, I had done that. When the big New Hampshire buck had fallen to my shot, I had tipped my hat to the sky and said, "Thanks. That's all I need for this year." And now here I was asking for another.

That night I had this dream.

I was in a torch-lit hall in a great castle that was filled with cornucopias spilling fruit. Deer and elk and caribou wandered about, nibbling at sacks of grain that were heaped in the corners of the room. Suddenly, a gorgeous woman swept into the hall. She wore a diaphanous gown and flowers in her golden hair and one abundant breast was proudly bared. I knew at once that I was in the presence of Mother Nature.

I explained that it turned out I needed another deer after all, despite my earlier statement that I had enough.

She smiled benevolently, her fine breasts lifting in the firelight, and led me down a corridor to a dimly lit anteroom. "I don't handle details like this myself, but you go in here and speak to my accountant," she said in a voice like Bambi's mother.

Seated at a wide desk was a thin, bald man wearing a green eyeshade. An enormous ledger was spread before him.

I stated my name and purpose and he ran his finger down the ledger entries, then looked up and stared at me with cold eyes.

"Mister Robinson," he blustered. "You need to make a deposit before you can make a withdrawal." Accountants have been telling me that all my life.

I awoke and lay in my sleeping bag, listening to the wind in the pines around the tent and the grating of river-born sheets of ice. "How do I make a deposit?" I asked myself.

I told my partners about my dream at breakfast, but they just traded knowing glances and edged away.

"A few days away from home and he's already dreaming about naked ladies," Jim Henry scoffed.

But that evening, when we regathered after another fruitless day in the woods, Jim announced, "I made my deposit."

He had been up in a tree overlooking the edge of a grassy alder swamp and had watched a doe swim across the river, enter the swamp, and reappear a few minutes later in the company of a 4-point buck.

"They were right in the open only 50 yards away," Jim related. "I was going to shoot the buck, but just then he mounted the doe and bred her. I thought it would be bad luck to shoot him out of the saddle, so I let him go."

He figured his gentlemanly forbearance should earn him credit in Mother Nature's big accounting book.

Apparently it worked, for the next day Jim was rewarded with a fat 6-pointer that came to his grunt call as if it had been sent.

Sitting in the woods the next day I saw a bald eagle soaring high in the sky. As I watched, the huge bird suddenly dropped out of the sky, came gliding in over the treetops, and perched in the top of the very tree beneath which I was sitting.

"Here I am in a virtual deer park, with tracks proving there are lots of deer all around me. I can't see a buck, yet the only eagle within miles chooses my tree to sit in. It defies the law of averages," I complained that night at supper.

"You haven't made your deposit yet," Jim reminded me.

The next day I watched a pair of otters playing on the ice, had a doe come so close I could have touched her with the muzzle of my rifle, and witnessed a red fox catching mice in a log-strewn cutover. The same day Jim saw a wolf trotting on the ice at the river's edge. Mother Nature was giving us a wonderful display, letting us see her rarest treasures. But no bucks.

On the sixth day the law of averages lost all credibility. At breakfast we had chosen a spot on the map and decided to hunt there for the day. It was about two miles away by canoe, in a remote piece of country that would be hard to reach without a boat. We made a mark on the map where we would beach the canoe and figured we should have that large area to ourselves.

We paddled in there quietly, and when we came to the spot we had marked on the map, I silently gestured the others to remain in the canoe while I climbed the high bank and took a peek at the surroundings. Then I scaled the bank and disappeared over the top.

I had taken only two steps when I was brought up short. Not 10 yards ahead a large buck lay on its side, its big antlers jutting up from the forest floor.

The deer was dead, shot through the heart, as it turned out. I put my finger in the deer's mouth. It was warm, freshly killed. Yet when I looked around the forest, I saw no sign of any living creature. Someone had shot a 9-point buck, killed it in its tracks, then walked away and left it at precisely the spot we had arbitrarily chosen on a map.

What are the chances of that happening? How many millions to one? Wouldn't it seem more likely that we should have seen one of the live bucks we were hunting for rather than zeroing in on a dead one?

The others went into the woods to hunt while I stayed behind to dress the buck. I wasn't going to claim it by putting my tag on it, but it seemed a shame to let it lie there and spoil, so I gutted it and hung the carcass over a log in plain sight, then went off to hunt.

Late that afternoon we regathered at the canoe. The only deer anyone had seen was the dead one that still lay over the log beside the canoe. No one had come along to claim it.

"We might as well tag it," Phil said. "No use leaving it here any longer. The law says a deer belongs to the man who tags it and nobody's come for it. It'll be dark soon."

Just then we heard people coming. Two young boys in orange hats were bobbing through the woods toward us. They went exactly to the spot where the buck had fallen. When they saw us gathered around the canoe with the buck's carcass, their faces fell.

I called them over.

"This must be your buck," I said. "We dressed him out so he wouldn't spoil, but we didn't tag him. He's yours."

The boys' relief was overwhelming. They couldn't stop thanking us and shaking our hands.

"I shot him from across the river," one of them said. "It was too deep to cross, so we had to go all the way home and get a boat and try to come back down here. It took all day. Our boat's just up around the bend. There's logs across the river and we couldn't bring it any closer.

"He disappeared when I shot, so I didn't know if I hit him or if he just dropped into a hollow and ran off," the boy continued.

"You hit him," I said. "Right through the heart."

"Wow!" the kid said. "I hit him there?"

I felt good as the boys dragged the buck away. I knew I'd made my deposit. Tomorrow would be the day.

Next morning we returned to the same spot and hunted separately all day. I cut out to the edge of the swamp and followed a ridge for a mile or so, moving quietly and slowly. Several times I saw deer, but none had horns.

Near the end of legal shooting time I was on the side of the ridge overlooking the swamp, working my way back toward the canoe. I stopped and leaned against a tree, watching.

Immediately, I heard footsteps in the frozen leaves. Then I saw deer hair coming my way between the thickly spaced trees. It was close. I raised my rifle and held on the edge of the tree that hid the deer's head from my view. When it appeared I scoped the antlers, made my decision, then dropped the crosshairs to a point just behind the buck's shoulder and fired.

This time we won't discuss the dimensions of the rack. Let's just say this was an eatin' deer of the first magnitude. Tender, plump, and absolutely legal—and it was the only living antlered deer I had seen in a week.

"Not a very impressive withdrawal," Jim said when I dragged it in. "Of course, your deposit wasn't worth much. You can't expect a lot of credit when all you did was not steal a kid's deer . . ."

We had one day to go and Phil's tag was still unused.

"I want to go back to that place again," Phil said. "I've been seeing tracks of an awful big buck in there, and I haven't made a withdrawal from my deer account in a long time."

Phil made a wide circle through the swamp. Around noon he was moving slowly along the edge of a frozen grassy prairie when he heard ice breaking up ahead. He stopped and a moment later saw a bunch of deer coming toward him.

"One was still making a lot of noise breaking through the ice on a little brook, and the others were bounding toward me in a bunch," he told us later. "I could see the big buck was with them, even though he was running with his head held low. His body was half again as big as the others. Then his head came up and I've never seen such a rack. It was 10 points anyway, maybe 12, with long tines and antler bases that were as thick as my wrist."

Phil shoots a sporty little 6mm Ruger single-shot rifle. He's comfortable with a single shot and light caliber because he never takes chance shots. When Phil squeezes the trigger, he has his target dead to rights. If he doesn't have a sure killing shot, he doesn't fire.

These deer had seen Phil at the same moment he saw them, and they leaped away tightly bunched. The big buck was right in the middle of them.

"I couldn't shoot," he told us. "But I had a darn good look at him, and he's all the buck I ever wanted. But I didn't have a clear shot—and then he was gone."

"I hope Mother Nature's accountant saw you pass up that shot," I said. "Sounds like you made a big deposit for next year."

5

CANOE HUNT AT FREEZE-UP TIME

The rain had stopped by the time we reached the river, but a cold, white mist was blowing through the valley, and it began to snow shortly after we started paddling. The flakes came in gusts that blew across the water in long streamers, and you could feel the temperature starting to slide.

Even the exertion of paddling was not enough to take the sting out of the cold wind, and by the time we reached the portage trail, the woods had turned white and we were all looking forward to getting the tents up and a fire in our portable stove. But first we had to deal with the next mile of rapids.

"The water's high after the rain," Jim Henry surmised. "We ought to be able to run it."

We walked the portage, scouted the rapids, and decided there was nothing to worry about—nothing you would have given a second thought to in the summer, but in northern Minnesota in November the idea of making a mistake and winding up in the water was gripping. It was like contemplating walking a two-foot-wide girder across the top of a railroad trestle. You could do it backwards if the girder were on the ground, but when you raise it dangerously high, your perspective changes and you worry.

One by one we dropped down through the fast water and were swept into the turn. The water quickened and waves lifted the bows of our canoes and licked along the rails. All four canoes were loaded with heavy winter camping gear, and you felt the extra weight when you dug with a paddle to pull the bow out of the path of rocks where whitewater growled. Finally, we shot out into the quiet pool at the bottom of the pitch, where all four canoes drifted side by side.

"That saved hours of lugging everything over the portage trail," Phil said. The run was behind us now and we could joke about it. There had been deer tracks on the portage trail. We found them in the mud beneath the skim of snow and saw that they led to a well-worn river crossing.

Half a mile beyond the rapids, we came to a wide bend in the river with a flat, grassy opening on one bank.

"Let's check that out," I suggested. It was sunset, and black clouds hung low in the West. Darkness was crowding us, and the cold was really beginning to bite.

On shore we determined that the flat was large enough for our big cook tent and the two sleeping tents. There was plenty of dead standing timber for firewood, and most of it was soft maple and swamp ash that would burn hot.

In back of the flat the hardwoods gave way to a low spruce-covered hill; along its base was as pretty a deer trail as we could hope to find. After a few minutes of scouting the four of us gathered back at the canoes.

"We're right in the middle of deer city," Jim said. We had all found abundant deer sign, including a large buck rub that gleamed in the failing light right at the edge of our clearing.

"We'll have two bucks hanging on the pole by nine tomorrow morning," Dean predicted. "Then we can celebrate in the afternoon, and kill two more the next morning. We can hunt ducks the rest of the week."

We cut a ridgepole for the big tent, erected it on a pair of criss-crossed saplings, and pegged the tent out taut. Then we cleared away the snow and set up the nylon sleeping tents. Our plan was to keep the big tent clear for cooking and eating and drying wet clothes. We'd keep our duffels and sleeping bags in the nylon tents.

The snow stopped falling by the time we had the tents up, so we stood outside and cooked thick T-bone steaks around a hardwood fire. We had buttery mashed potatoes and vegetables and a bottle of sour mash bourbon to help sweeten the tea. I had shot a partridge while we were paddling, and we sautéed the breasts in butter and flamed them in bourbon as hors d'oeuvres.

"We're gonna get 'em," Dean kept saying. "New snow and we're right in the middle of where they live."

We awoke the next morning to rain. The light snow covering had disappeared and mist rose from the ground and hung in shrouds over the river. We ate our eggs and bacon and assured each other that it didn't matter, we didn't need the snow. We were sure to get one buck this morning, anyway.

By 8 o'clock it was pouring. We had split four ways and gone into the woods at daylight, and now we were scattered on the hillside hunkering under anything that would keep the rain off. It was miserable and cold, but the deer sign was promising.

Below me were three deer trails that crossed in a glade. From my vantage point, I could see several buck scrapes close to the junction. I ached to see a deer. I knew just how he would look. I could picture him silently entering the scene. He would stop right *there*. I could imagine the wide, dark rack, and the crosshairs centered just behind his shoulder, a third of the way up from the bottom line of his chest. I would slip off the safety, breathe out, and squeeze. I was ready.

Paddling into a remote place and hunting out of tents brings on a certain feeling of entitlement. I felt that I had earned a deer. We had worked hard to reach this remote territory, and we were living with the deer. Now it was just a matter of time until a buck and I came to the same place at the same time. Then it's who sees who first. I was ready, but no deer came.

At noon I quit and went back to the tent. It seemed like a good time to cut a load of firewood, stoke up the woodstove, and build a dining table while I dried out. The others straggled into camp about the same time with similar ideas. No one had seen anything. Lots of sign but no deer. All game was holed up against the weather, and it seemed wise for us to follow suit.

In a couple of hours we cut and stacked enough firewood to last a week, then built a table and a drying rack. We crowded in around the hot stove and, as steam rose from our wet clothes, we ate hot soup and cheese and crackers and drank steaming mugs of rose hip tea to build a vitamin C buffer against catching colds.

The rain turned to snow around 3 o'clock and that pleased us. "They'll move this evening for sure," Dean opined. "They've got to feed ahead of this storm."

The woods were quiet underfoot as we drifted out to hunt. The snow and wet leaves made no sound. The snow was sifting down harder now, muffling our movements. The wind was strengthening out of the North. It sighed in the spruce tops, and the driving snow made a sound like sand against the hardwood trees. Only the slant of the snow gave any sense of direction. Not even a gray squirrel moved that day.

"Hunting shouldn't be easy," Dean pronounced at dinner. "It wouldn't feel as good if you could just go out and knock one over."

"Cut the crap," Phil growled. "I wish we had all four hung up right now. That'd give me a good enough feeling."

Tomorrow would be the day, we told each other. We had learned where the trails were and where they led. In the morning, with new snow and some fresh tracks to work, we'd get into them.

But it was still snowing next morning, and back in the woods there were no tracks. The woods lay still. Nothing was moving but us hunters. The hunted were probably bedded back in the thickest stuff out of the wind, waiting for the storm to break. There was also the possibility that the deer had moved out ahead of the storm and migrated to their winter range.

The snow continued for three days and the temperature continued to drop. The river froze along the shore, and big chunks of ice came down through the rapids and began to jam and freeze together at the bend below our camp. In the woods the snow was now knee deep. No one had seen a deer or a fresh track since the snow began.

"It's like the earth just swallowed them up," Phil said at the end of a long day spent crawling through the thickest cover searching for some fresh sign of deer. "They were here when we arrived, but not now."

Once we heard shooting in the distance and thought, well, someone's found a deer. But the next day I met a hunter in the woods, and he said the shooting had been a member of his group who had gotten lost.

"He kept on shooting and getting answers," the hunter told me. "Finally, he met the other shooter and it turned out the other guy was lost, too. They spent the night in the woods together. We tracked them and got them out this morning. You've gotta be careful around here; you can get lost easily."

It was funny country, all right. Rich iron deposits made our compasses unreliable and we navigated pretty much by feel, trying to keep a sense of where the river was at all times. The river lay to the west and north of the area we were hunting, and there was an old overgrown railroad bed a mile to the east. The direction not to go was south. You could go south for 20 miles and not hit anything.

The higher hills were bald on top, and it was stirring to go up there and look around. As far as you could see in all directions there were only low hills covered with aspen and spruce.

We had no thermometer to tell us how cold it was, but the hairs froze in our nostrils when we breathed and the insides of the un-heated sleeping tents were frosted with rime. One morning was par-ticularly cold. We had to thaw our frozen boots by the stove before we could pound our feet down into them. Our outer clothes froze stiff as boards when we hunted.

At night we listened to the grating sound of ice moving slowly down the river and knew our time for hunting was running out.

"We better get our deer soon, or we're going to get frozen in here," Jim warned that morning. "Any more heavy snow on top of that floating ice and the river's going to freeze across." The river was already frozen several yards out from the shore, and the water had the viscous quality of syrup when you swirled a paddle through it.

Next morning the clouds cleared and the sunrise was pink. In the woods you could feel a difference. There was life here again. Squirrels came out and greeted the sun. Fisher tracks cut through the woods with their familiar two by two pattern. That morning the coyotes set up a yammering on a nearby hilltop, announcing the re-sumption of the hunt. And now there were deer tracks.

It seemed every deer in the woods was on the move. After four days of trackless snow, this new display was stunning. There were deer tracks everywhere. I crossed a dozen sets of tracks between the tent and the old railroad grade.

It was soon clear that the deer were moving out. Every track was headed south, toward a huge tract of spruce forest that lay 10 miles away and was renowned as a winter deer range. If we didn't get deer today, we could forget about tomorrow, for the deer would all be gone.

Late that morning I heard a shot from Dean's direction, but there was no follow-up set of signal shots asking for help so I stayed where I was until evening and then headed back to camp. I had seen only two deer, both antlerless. The sky was clear but it was very cold.

I found Dean and Phil in camp stringing up a 4-pointer. "It was a short drag," Dean said. "I figured I'd let you guys stay out hunting, so I didn't signal for help."

As daylight left the sky we fired up the stove and got dinner ready, waiting for Jim. Darkness came and he still had not shown up. We fired signal shots but got no answer.

"Gonna be a cold night to stay in the woods," Dean said.

"Not much we can do but wait for morning and track him," I said. "If he's lost he can backtrack himself when it gets light."

Just then the tent flap was yanked open and there stood Jim. His hat was gone, his hair was sticking up and full of spruce needles, he was red-faced and sweaty, and his coat was steaming. But he was smiling and he held up a plastic bag with a deer's heart and liver in it.

"Ten-pointer!" he roared. "I've been dragging him all after-noon."

There is a wonderfully elemental feeling when a difficult hunt ends successfully. The satisfaction you get from dragging a big buck out through the snow toward camp, even when it's someone else's deer, is enough of a reward. The next morning we helped Jim drag the big buck from where he left it the rest of the way to his canoe. He loaded it and began paddling upstream toward camp. The ice crackled as the bow of his canoe sliced through it, and up on the bald hilltop the coyotes were yammering again. The deer's big rack was jutting up in the front of Jim's canoe. The rigors and disappointments of the past few days were forgotten. It didn't even seem cold now. If you were a deer hunter, this was just where you wanted to be.

Now the challenge was to get out before the river froze.

We packed hurriedly at dawn. Everything was frozen stiff and the loads that had fitted so nicely in the canoes when we started our journey now stuck out at funny angles and had to be pounded into place. The frozen cooking tent weighed half again its normal weight, and we had added more than 300 pounds of deer carcasses to the load.

We had to load the canoes on the shelf of ice that had formed along the shore, then get into them and use the paddles to pole the canoes across the widening band of ice and into the water.

"We'll just take it easy and drift along with the plates of floating ice," Jim said. "We'll be all right if we just drift and don't try to increase our forward speed."

We drifted along like that for almost a mile, but we could feel the speed of the current slowing as the river widened. The ice was now wide along the shore, leaving only a narrowing channel for us to pass through. When we drifted around the next wide bend the scene ahead was stark. As far as we could see, the river was frozen all the way across, and the ice was covered with snow.

We had chosen this section of river because it was remote. No bridges crossed it for more than 20 miles. We figured we still had at least 12 miles to go before we reached our trucks.

Our canoes slid up against the jammed ice and stopped.

"The current was fast where we camped because we were just below those rapids," Jim said. "We should have realized that the ice would jam where the current slowed."

We progressed at a snail's pace for the next six hours. The man in the lead canoe would pole his canoe up onto the ice as far as it would go, then stand up and jump down hard in the hull, cracking the ice beneath and allowing the canoe to be pushed forward about half a canoe length at a time. We took turns being icebreaker, with the other canoes following behind.

"Good thing we have Kevlar and Royalex hulls," Jim said. "You couldn't do this with canvas or aluminum hulls. They wouldn't slide."

Nevertheless, our efforts were of diminishing value as the ice became thicker as the current beneath us continued to slow. In six hours of hard work we made only a little more than two miles. We knew the river would tighten up even more that night. It appeared we were stranded. Once more, it began to snow.

Maps are sometimes wrong. Luckily for us, our map failed to show that an old railroad grade that once crossed the river near where we finally came to shore was being used to access a lonely cabin. The cabin was empty and covered with snow, but we were delighted to find that the the old railroad grade which led to it was rutted by vehicles. At the edge of darkness we started hiking down the rutted road away from the river, leaving the canoes and gear heaped on shore under tarps.

"Whoever owns this cabin drives in here," Phil said. "It may be a long walk, but we can hike out on his tracks and drive our trucks back in here to pick up our stuff."

Our luck had turned, and now it ran in our direction full bore. In a quarter mile we came to a second cabin, and this one had smoke curling from the chimney and a 4-wheel-drive truck parked in the yard.

We found the owner inside skinning a beaver.

"Come in, boys," he said. "You look frozen. Have a drink. Stand here by the stove." The cabin was deliciously warm and smelled of woodsmoke and bacon, and oil lamps lit the room. We were home safe now, with a big deer, a little deer and, even though the river was plugged up tight, it didn't matter anymore.

"I'll take you out to your trucks," the trapper said. "Soon as you get warmed up. Have some more cognac."

A week earlier you couldn't have told any of us that civilization would feel so good. Now, in this warm, lamp-lit room, with the certainty that we could bring our trucks here to pick up our outfit, our thoughts turned homeward, and we couldn't wait to get rolling down the road.

"All of a sudden I miss my wife," Dean said.

"Me, too," Jim said. "When I get home, the second thing I'm going to do is show my wife that deer."

6

ISLAND
OF THE
DEER

North of the natural limit of whitetail deer range and apparently too far east as well, Anticosti Island, 40 miles off the coast of Quebec, has one of the densest deer herds in North America. Depending on the severity of recent winters, deer on this narrow 134-mile-long island fluctuate in number between about 70,000 to more than 100,000. They continue to attain numbers that approach the carrying capacity of the range, allowing a two-deer-per-person bag limit and a season that extends from August into December.

Anticosti itself stands squarely in the center of the broad mouth of the St. Lawrence River, halfway between the eastern end of the Gaspé peninsula and the southern tip of Labrador. It is a low, rolling island, cut by short, swift rivers to which Atlantic salmon and sea-run brook trout return each summer. A thick blanket of spruce/fir forest covers the island, interspersed with low hardwood ridges. Generations of lumbermen have built logging roads and skidder trails that crisscross the island and give hunters access to thousands of square miles of prime deer habitat.

Anticosti is too far offshore for deer or other land animals to spread there naturally. The island's best-in-the-world whitetail population is entirely the product of 220 deer that were trapped on the nearby Gaspé peninsula and brought to Anticosti by Henri Menier, a wealthy French chocolate manufacturer who purchased the island in 1896 to establish a private game preserve.

The island was barren of game species when Menier acquired it. During the years he owned it, Menier successfully introduced deer, moose, beaver, muskrat, rabbits, silver foxes, otters, fishers, and frogs to Anticosti. Introductions of bison and elk were also attempted, but failed.

Even though the island suffers winter extremes as severe as anywhere that whitetails exist, and offers food sources which are no more nutritious than many regions where deer do poorly, Anticosti's deer maintain their abundance because the harvest is carefully controlled. Such management is made that much easier because Anticosti has no predators that attack deer—no coyotes, wolves, bobcats, lynx, or domestic dogs.

In the 30 years that Anticosti was owned by the Menier family the island became a wildlife paradise. Its outstanding game animal resources were later maintained by a series of pulp and paper company owners who operated on the island until the 1960s, when it became unprofitable to conduct forestry operations there.

Today Anticosti Island is maintained entirely for hunting and fishing. The log lodges built by the lumber companies for the entertainment of company guests and employees are now operated by a government corporation and are open to the public on a reservation basis. Five additional lodges are operated by private owners to accommodate sportsmen in a previously inaccessible area in the eastern portion of the island.

Having heard stories about this extraordinary deer hunter's Valhalla, I booked a hunt for the last four days of the season at Jupiter 24, a log lodge two miles up the beautiful Jupiter River, roughly in the center of the island.

The early morning flight from Montreal took off in heavy rain, but it was snowing by the time we reached Quebec City. When we arrived in Sept Illes, 450 miles east, a full scale blizzard was blowing, and all chances of flying in to Anticosti that day were dashed.

We spent a comfortable night in the Auberge des Goveurneur in Sept Illes as snow piled up outside. By morning it was a foot deep and still falling. Our flight to Anticosti was canceled for another day.

Early in the afternoon, however, the snow stopped briefly, so we joined four other anxious hunters to see if we could put together a charter for the short flight out to the island.

"Let's try to go while we can," one of the hunters advised. "If it starts snowing again the scheduled flight for tomorrow will be canceled, too."

We piled into a little six-seater and flew out to Anticosti at 200 feet altitude between lowering clouds and a sea fog that was building up on the water below.

"I'd never fly like this on business," one of the hunters said. "But I've hunted Anticosti before and I've always said I'd do *anything* to hunt there again. It's that good."

We traveled in a chartered schoolbus from the little airport at Port Menier to our lodge. It was snowing hard again.

It was still snowing the next morning, and our guide, Normand Galant, opined that the deer would not move until the storm subsided. "You're lucky you got here," he said. "When this storm breaks the deer will have to move."

Nonetheless, Normand took us out in his Ford pickup to see the country and entertained us with the kinds of stories that fill you with high anticipation on the first day in new territory.

Because of our delayed arrival and the loss of the first day's hunt due to the snowstorm, I would have only two days to hunt.

"What do you think, Normand?" I asked. "Will there be time to get two good bucks?"

His answer was positive.

"You will have the chance to kill two big bucks," he replied. "But you will have to shoot straight and not make mistakes.

"For big bucks, the later in the season, the more you will see," he told me. "By now most of the does have been bred and are back in the swamps. They don't want the bucks now. They're hiding from them. So the bucks move all the time looking for does that are not bred yet. Now is when the biggest bucks move most. They travel all the time, and don't eat.

"They lose maybe 20 pounds from too much chasing females, too much hanky-pank," he said.

"Too bad we can't lose weight like that," I commented.

"We can!" Normand replied. "Just look at me."

All that first day I walked through heavy falling snow, scouring the thick woods for a bedded buck, but I saw none. Late in the afternoon the storm broke and a red sunset lit the sky.

"Tomorrow is the day," Normand assured me. "The day after a storm; that is when they move."

We started out next day before daylight and drove to the hunting zone that was reserved for us. On Anticosti each pair of hunters is assigned to an exclusive zone measuring at least five miles by five miles in which no other hunters will be that day. There are so many hunting zones that sometimes weeks go by between days a zone is hunted.

"Nobody's hunted here for more than two weeks," Normand said when he dropped me off at the head of a trail. I had chosen to hunt alone, without a guide's assistance.

"Just follow that trail until you see a big beaver swamp maybe two miles in," Normand instructed. "There are always does around there, and the big bucks will be looking for them."

From the moment I stepped into the woods I was among deer tracks. The deer had been moving all night and the woods were tracked up like a warren. Deer tracks crossed the trail every few yards, and other deer had walked in the trail itself. I moved in a state of suspended animation, studying the scene for a line that didn't quite fit. The deep, fluffy snow muffled any sound of my approach. The wind was still. The advantages were mine.

In an hour I had moved only half a mile along the trail. I had seen two does cross the trail, but no bucks. Once I had felt eyes on me and froze, studying the dark growth of the snow-laden fir forest. Then I saw him, a spike buck that had spotted my movement but had not caught my scent. For a moment we held each other's gaze, then he turned and trotted stiff-kneed across the trail and disappeared into the darkness of the black forest.

I kept creeping along, paralleling the hunting trail so that I could move from tree to tree, staying in the shadows, keen and expectant. When I had gone almost a mile into the woods, my eye caught movement on the top of a small knoll that lay in sunlight up ahead. I froze. There it was once more.

As I watched a thicket of twigs beside a short snow-burdened balsam fir, I saw a short brown object twitch again. Was it a squirrel? Now there was a greater movement, and suddenly I got a clear view of a deer's head. The twitching object was his ear. As he turned his head a wide antler rack stained the color of tea caught the early morning sunlight. Now I saw the brilliant eyes, the glistening black nose, the gray face, but I could not see the deer's body. Then I spotted a doe bedded a few yards from the buck. They had not seen me and there was no wind to carry my scent their way.

Slowly I dropped into the snow, scrunched up beside a yellow birch trunk, and raised my rifle. The buck's head and neck were fully visible through the scope, but his body was hidden from view by the deep snow in which he lay. His antlers were thick, and I counted eight long tines. I screwed the Leupold variable scope up to full power, rested the rifle on my knee, placed the crosshairs on the buck's white throat patch, let out my breath, and squeezed the trigger.

At the shot the doe bounded away, her tail flagging, but the buck disappeared. Had he dived backwards into a hollow I couldn't see?

I plowed through the snow, climbing the steep side of the knoll on which he had been bedded, and peeked over the top. My buck lay dead in his bed. He had not moved, but just dropped his head into the snow.

The buck was a nice 2–1/2-year-old 8-pointer that would dress out at about 165 pounds. Not a wall hanger, but a fine example of the kind of bucks most often killed on Anticosti. I field-dressed the buck, then dragged the carcass out to the road.

"You don't have to pull them out," Normand admonished me when he drove up in the truck. "Just leave your deer where you shoot it and go hunt for another. It's my job to pull them out for you."

He felt the buck's ribs and loins, squeezing with his fingers.

"Still pretty fat," he said. "He'll be good to eat."

Normand then drove me to a wild section of my hunting zone where there were no roads. Instead, he drove his Ford pickup into a narrow stream bed that consisted of flat slabs of limestone, and plunged downstream. For a mile or more we jounced along in water that was often deep enough to flood the floorboards of the truck. In places he drove through water I thought was deep enough to flood the engine. Steam billowed up from the hood and fogged the windshield. Our tailpipe gurgled and blew bubbles.

"Anticosti car wash," Normand chuckled.

Eventually he climbed out of the stream bed and we took off through unplowed snow, driving on stump-filled log skidder trails until we drew near a little bunch of knobby hills.

"Go in there," Normand told me. "Go slow and look everywhere. There's big bucks living in those hills and nobody's hunted here."

Again I entered a Christmas card scene full of snow and evergreens. There were deer tracks everywhere, and no tracks of other hunters.

"Lots of hunters come to Anticosti and only hunt from the roads," Normand had told me. "Most of them don't want to go far into the woods. Very few hunters want to hunt alone far back in the woods like this. You'll find a big one here, for sure."

I worked my way up the side of the first knob and crawled into a thicket from which I could peer over the top and survey what lay ahead without being seen. It was mostly cutover country with pockets of cover surrounded by openings. I immediately spotted three deer browsing along the edge of a beaver pond a quarter mile below me. The scope showed that they were does without consorts, and their calm attitude indicated there were no bucks nearby pestering them.

I continued poking along amongst the little knobby hills, peeking around shoulders into protected pockets and over hilltops that gave me clear views of the hillsides that lay ahead. Several times I spotted deer bedded in the sun, but they always proved to be does with fawns.

Then, late in the afternoon, as the lowering sun lengthened the shadows and added a golden richness to the snow, I topped a little rise and saw a big doe lift from her bed and move off into the trees.

No wind bore my scent toward her, and only the top of my head showed over the little knob, so I was sure I had not caused her to move. I slipped around the shoulder of the knob and dropped lower into the darkness of the forest. Then I saw the doe again.

She was sleek and fat, and there was no fawn trailing her. I remember Normand saying this was the kind of deer he liked best for meat.

"These you can eat with a spoon," he had commented.

The doe was restless. She stared off to the left and waggled her ears. I wondered if maybe she had a fawn with her after all.

But then I recalled what Normand had cautioned.

"If you see a single doe, watch out," he'd told me. "That's the kind the big bucks go for. This late in the season a moving single doe is a signal that a buck may be following her."

The doe was still staring off to the left and now I was, too. I wanted to see what she was looking at. Then I caught movement in a thin space between two spruces. I focused my gaze there, and suddenly an enormous buck materialized in the gloom. His antlers curved widely out beyond his ears, and long tines swooped upward. His neck, swollen with the passion of the rut, stood up from his shoulders like a sturdy log.

He moved behind the thin screen of a wind-toppled birch tree, and for a moment I lost sight of him. Then I saw him again, down on his belly, crawling under a horizontal tree trunk, tipping his antlers to the side to keep them from getting caught. He was less than 60 yards away and my rifle was up and the scope was on him as he came out from under the fallen tree and stepped into the open. When he turned to stare at the doe, I settled the crosshairs behind his shoulder and fired.

"Oh, he's a grand one," Normand said when he came to where he had heard me shoot. He examined the 10-pointer, and measured the rack at 23 inches. "That's the biggest rack in camp, for sure," he exclaimed. "This buck will make everyone want to hunt farther back in the woods."

Two shots, two bucks and both good ones, in a single day's hunt! I couldn't imagine deer hunting ever being better than that.

Deer hunting on Anticosti is so good that every hunter gets a chance to kill two deer. Not every hunter kills two, and some go home with smaller deer than they had wished for, but those are hunters who either fail to kill a large buck when they get the chance, or who shoot the first deer they see, not trusting that they will see bigger deer if they hold off.

I had never hunted deer out of an organized camp before going to Anticosti, having always hunted on my own either from my cabin or from tent camps I erected with my own party of hunters in some public forest.

Now I'm spoiled. I must admit I liked coming in at night to a warm camp, a hot shower, a drink by the fire, good meals that some-one else cooked, and a comfortable bed up off the ground.

Comfort aside, however, it is the hunting that is so extra special at Anticosti. I have never seen so much deer sign, or had so much prime deer habitat to myself. Knowing that you have an exclusive hunting zone in which no other hunters will be competing for the deer enables you to hunt the way you want. You can expect the deer to be following their natural habits, not running off, scared by other hunters.

After Anticosti, I'm going to be awfully hard to please anywhere else.

7

HORSEBACK DEER HUNT

Rolie Devost is not a man you'd peg as a horseman, but you'd have thought he was an old-time saddle tramp when he spotted that big buck scrootched down in a spruce thicket waiting for our horses to pass by. Rolie reined in, rolled out of the saddle, and pulled his rifle out of the scabbard in one smooth motion. As his feet hit the ground he darted into the woods, dropped a single cartridge into the chamber, stepped up to a stump, and fired.

I hadn't seen anything.

"Qué pasa?" I blurted. We were trying to speak French on this trip, but I couldn't remember how to ask what was going on in French, so I said it in Spanish.

"Le grand buck," Rolie said. "Il est morte!"

It was an 8-pointer, a nice one that dressed out at about 185 pounds. From his seat atop his horse Rolie had seen its antlers sticking out of the sides of a little Christmas tree the buck had been using to screen itself from our sight as we rode by. "What a view you get from the top of a horse!" Rolie said. "I wouldn't have seen that deer if I was on foot."

We had ridden to the Riviere aux Plats tent camp from a lodge on the Chicotte River about five miles away and were now based at the edge of a territory approximately five miles wide and ten miles long. We were to be the only hunters in that area for the duration of our stay.

A few rough trails had been hacked through the black spruce forest giving us access to a mix of open peat bogs, forested ridges, and windswept coastal beaches where deer sometimes go to eat seaweed. When there were no trails to our far-flung hunting destinations we rode in the wide limestone bed of the Riviere aux Plats itself.

With the horses blowing jets of steam in the frosty morning air, we rode out after breakfast each morning, following the winding riverbed and fording the river back and forth several times in every mile. Although we rode mostly at a walking pace, the sure-footed horses were quick steppers and miles passed quickly.

When a chosen hunting place was reached, we'd tie the horses and leave them in the care of Claude, the wrangler, while one of us went off to hunt with Alain, our guide, and the other two went off separately to hunt alone on foot.

The Riviere aux Plats Camp is on Anticosti Island in Quebec. It was mid-November, the peak of the rut, and bucks were on the move all day and night. Their drag-toed tracks went everywhere, and showed clearly in the trace of snow that the low, gray clouds replenished nightly.

"It's the perfect time for using rattling antlers," Alain told us. "Use them every time you stop, then watch for ten or fifteen minutes. If a buck is nearby, you can make him come to you."

I rattled in a nice 5-point buck the very first morning. I had just come to a place where budworm had killed off a few acres of spruce trees leaving a ragged edge of forest and a wide opening with clumps of new spruce coming in. I picked a dark spot on the forest edge to hide in, then clapped the antlers together and put on a 60-second twisting and rattling performance.

When I repeated my act a few minutes later, I heard a twig snap off to my right, and then the buck bounded into view. He slammed to a stop less than 40 yards away, presenting a clear broadside shot.

My other hunting partner, Jim, killed a 6-point buck that same morning. He had been using a grunt call sporadically and had seen nothing approaching, but when he began moving again he ran head-on into a buck that had been coming to his calls.

The horses we rode were mixed bloods with big feet that never slipped, long legs that kept our stirrups above the water when we forded deep places, and big, strong backs that carried us uphill and down with ease. They were nice, calm farm horses from the Gaspé peninsula, with especially friendly dispositions, and they understood French, not English.

When I said "Attaboy" in my horse's ear after he bore me safely across a fast, deep run place in the river the first morning, he just plodded on as if he hadn't heard me. When I told him "C'est bon cheval" instead, his ears perked up and he turned his head to give me an appreciative eye.

And then there was Barbie, the packhorse.

Barbie was one of those horses you just instantly take a shine to. She was a cross between a large pony and a draft horse. Built like a barrel with short legs and a broad back and hefty hindquarters, she had a moose-black hide and a bushy blond mane, tail, and forelock that gave her a stylish look. The geldings we rode all wanted to stand next to Barbie whenever we stopped, and somehow we all found an extra half sandwich for Barbie at lunchtime.

She was enormously strong. Her wooden panniers, packsaddle, and the sack of grain she carried for the horses' noontime feed made a 150-pound burden to begin with. When we added our two 165-pound bucks to her load that first morning, Barbie just shrugged, tossed her head, and followed us out through the woods, stepping over high logs, plodding through knee-deep peat bogs, and jauntily twitching her hindquarters as she skidded down steep, slippery slopes.

We never had to drag a deer at all. Whenever one of us shot a buck, somebody would go get Barbie and bring her all the way to the kill sight, and we'd load the deer right there.

I loved the horseback aspect of this hunt, but it's not for everyone. The riding does take time away from hunting. Each day we would ride for at least an hour and sometimes up to two hours before we got off to hunt the area that the guide had chosen. If you like horseback riding, the long morning and evening rides through the woods and winding river courses add extra enjoyment to the six or seven hours that you spend each day hunting on your feet, but if horseback riding is not your bag, the time spent riding could be bothersome.

Hunters are not permitted to shoot from horseback, but if you spot a buck while you are riding, as in Rolie's case, it is perfectly okay to get off your horse and go after the deer on foot. The horses are used to close gunfire and are trained to wait patiently for their rider to return.

The secret to attracting bucks with rattling antlers and grunt calls is being heard. If a buck doesn't hear your sounds, he can't respond to them. Anticosti is a great place to learn to use rattling horns and grunt calls because with a population of about 105,000 deer, the island averages more than 40 deer per square mile. Each hunter has a large exclusive zone in which there are no other hunters to disturb the deer. The dense deer population improves the chances that your efforts will be heard by a buck, and the lack of disturbance makes it more likely that a buck will respond to your efforts.

Anticosti guides are all great believers in using rattling horns and grunt calls, so you also have the advantage of seeing how the experts do it.

Our guide, Alain, had a quiet sort of sporadic rattling style that was very different from the noisy clatter, bashing, and branch-breaking that I find successful, and I was intrigued watching him at work.

Alain would begin with a quiet clunk of the antlers, then put pressure on the interlocked horns and twist them several times at intervals that were often seconds apart. In between these alternating clunks and twists he would pull the antlers apart while twisting them to make the sound of antlers separating under pressure. Then he would pound the antler butts on the frozen ground as if they were the hooves of two deer pushing hard against each other.

"I make sound like pushing contest, not sword fight," he said.

During pauses, he would sometimes make a soft grunt or two. On occasion he would rake the antlers on the rough bark of a rotting stump or knock over some piece of standing deadwood to make an extra loud sound that would carry farther.

Alain was doing this one frosty morning in a thick spruce glade after a new snowfall. We had ridden out a few miles, tied the horses on the riverbank, and hunted on foot up into a bunch of little forested hills and open bogs where deer sign was abundant.

Alain had been rattling and grunting for several minutes, and I was standing a few feet to his left watching for movement.

Sometimes bucks rush in noisily and you can hear them coming long before you see them, but this one came in like a ghost. I never heard a sound or saw any movement. Suddenly he was just there, a nice 8-pointer, staring at me from behind a little spruce tree about 35 yards away, and I dropped him with a single shot fired through the spruce branches at the spot where I calculated his chest had to be.

The varied terrain on Anticosti makes it possible to hunt in several ways. I tend to hunt the thick spruce forests where visibility is limited but where you have a good chance of rattling a buck in to close range. I like to stillhunt, and the thick spruces offer opportunities to slip around quietly, peeking here and there.

For hunters who prefer longer, more open shots, there are numerous boggy heaths covered with grass and small hardwood shrubs where you can take a stand and wait for deer to move into view. Or you can go to the beach and sit amidst a pile of driftwood and wait for deer to come to the coast to feed on seaweed, then attempt to stalk to within shooting range.

Some of the largest bucks killed on Anticosti have been taken by expert marksmen who made successful long-range shots at prime bucks that were spotted in unapproachable positions far out on open peat bogs.

You don't need horses to hunt successfully on Anticosti Island, but if you like horses, they add a certain element to deer hunting that is missing without them. Horses are characters and they can be pretty funny to have around.

Take Jim's horse King.

One morning Jim was giving King a friendly scratch behind the ears before mounting up when the horse suddenly swung his head around and chomped down on the bubble compass Jim had pinned to his jacket.

"Damn horse just ate my compass," Jim croaked. "He swallowed it."

For the rest of the week, whenever we returned to the tied horses, we'd see Jim with a stick poking around in the manure King had dropped while we were off hunting.

"I need that compass," Jim complained. "He's got to pass it sometime."

But Jim never did find his compass.

"If that horse starts heading North all the time, I'll know why," he said. "We ought to rename him Polaris."

WHY ANTICOSTI HUNTING IS SO SUCCESSFUL

Anticosti Island's unmatchable deer hunting success rate (above 1.7 per hunter annually) continues year after year due to a high deer density combined with an unusually high deer visibility factor.

Hunters see more deer moving during daylight hours on Anticosti because the conditions that cause mainland deer to restrict their daytime movement or migrate to other regions do not exist here.

There are no deer predators on Anticosti to make the deer nervous—no coyotes, wolves, black bears, or dogs. Because Anticosti is an island (38 miles wide in the middle and 134 miles long) surrounded by a broad barrier of water, no deer predators can reach it.

Hunters take around 4,000 deer per year on Anticosti during a season that runs from September 1 to the end of November, but all hunting is controlled by licensed outfitters who have divided their hunting territories into zones where each hunter has several square miles entirely to himself. Because of this, there is never enough hunting pressure to spook the deer or limit normal daytime deer movements.

Anticosti Island maintains a totally natural deer herd averaging 100,000 animals living in a totally wild condition. There are no feeding stations, no enclosures, and no artificially provoked deer activity.

Anticosti's climate favors successful deer survival. The island's location in the Gulf of St. Lawrence moderates the cold, improving winter deer survival. The limestone base of the island encourages a rich growth of nourishing vegetation which is not common in most spruce/fir forests farther south and the sea provides an additional winter food supply in the form of seaweeds that litter the hundreds of miles of beaches bordering the forest.

8

HOW
TO
STILLHUNT

The term "stillhunting" is misleading because a stillhunter does not just stand still, he moves; but he moves at a slow, careful pace, and stands still for long periods of time watching and listening. His motions are almost undetectable.

The stillhunter's rule is: "If you're seeing deer tails, you're moving too fast." Those are deer that saw you before you saw them. Likewise, if you must look down to watch your footing, you're moving too fast. Instead, plan your next few steps before you leave a position, then keep your eyes up, alert to your surroundings, while you make your move. At your new position, stop again for a long time before making your next short move.

Your movements will be least noticeable if you stay in the shadows. When you stop to watch, stop in the shadow of a large tree.

When you move, follow a route that avoids bright, sunlit places. Stay below ridgelines so that you do not silhouette yourself against the skyline.

To move quietly in dry or frozen leaves, keep your weight on the foot that is under you while you place your advancing foot into the leaves heel first. Roll your weight forward on to the advancing foot after your heel is steadied. Once your weight is fully on that foot, begin to advance the other foot.

The crunching sounds that are made under your feet don't carry far. But watch out for dry snags that can catch your foot or clothing and break with a loud snap above the ground. Sounds made above the ground send out loud reports that can be heard for long distances.

Try not to bump against saplings. Their upper branches shake and rattle, and the sound and motion can warn deer of your approach.

When you are stopped, study your surroundings, looking for anything that doesn't quite fit. You may not see a whole deer, but you may spot part of one—the bend of a deer's hind leg, the straight horizontal line of its back, an ear sticking out from behind a tree.

Pay particular attention to the edges of thick cover on raised knolls, for those are favorite bedding places. When bedded, deer often keep their bodies obscured. Only the neck and head may be visible above ground level.

Tracks always tell where a deer has been, but sometimes they also predict where a deer is going.

If a track suddenly turns downwind and heads uphill, it signals that the deer is moving toward a bedding area from which it can both watch its backtrail and catch the scent of any predator that may be following.

Stop where you are and assess the situation. Then back up the way you came for at least 100 yards. Now carefully move downwind for about 100 yards, so that you will no longer be on the deer's back-trail. Study your surroundings carefully.

Where is the nearest patch of cover on raised ground? That is probably where your deer is bedded.

Using all your skills as a stillhunter, move toward that spot with every sense at full alert. Expect to find the deer at the edge of heavy cover in a place that offers a view of its backtrail and an opportunity to see and scent anything that is following its tracks.

Two or three stillhunters moving as a team can be very effective. One hunter follows the track while the second and third hunters act as wing-men, following parallel courses 100 or more yards on either side of the track-follower. The wing-men should keep the track-follower just barely in sight so that they can see his directional changes and stay parallel to the track when it turns. If there are only two hunters, the wing-men should parallel the track on the upwind side because, more often than not, deer run upwind when jumped.

Successful stillhunting depends upon stealth. Every move you make must be accomplished quietly.

Your clothing must not rattle or snap when it comes into contact with stems and branches. When you move, your clothing should not rustle so loudly that it interferes with your ability to hear small sounds.

The quietest clothing you can wear is made of wool, cotton, or polyester fleece. Wool pants, wool shirt, wool jacket, cotton and wool long underwear, and a polyester fleece vest for extra warmth make the best combination for stillhunting.

9

HUNTING MIGRATORY WHITETAILS

When snow reaches their knees, whitetails move out. Whenever it occurs in northern or mountainous areas, knee-deep snow triggers a general whitetail migration that causes widely scattered bands of deer to move into winter congregations, often traveling many miles to do so.

From a hunter's standpoint, this shift, which can happen within a 24-hour period, means that a large portion of what has been considered good deer country until this moment suddenly empties.

Whitetails are not generally thought of as migratory animals, yet during these shifts from summer to winter range, deer travel more than 20 miles. While migrations of five to 10 miles are common in most states, telemetry studies in Minnesota have tabulated deer migrations of as much as 55 miles there. Deer in the Upper Peninsula of Michigan are known to move as much as 32 miles to reach their winter range, and whitetail migrations of 25 to 35 miles have been recorded in Montana and in the mountains of western South Dakota. Even in the South, whitetail migrations of five to six miles are normal when knee-deep snow falls in the mountains of northwestern Georgia and western North Carolina.

Even if the deer move only a mile from where they have been, you are not going to see them unless you move, too.

Hunters often fail to recognize the significance of these migratory shifts because they usually occur at the very end of hunting season or after the season is over. When deep snow comes during hunting season and an area that had previously shown a normal amount of deer sign suddenly shows none, it is easy to misunderstand what has happened. You may think that the deer are holed up someplace refusing to move, when actually the sign has disappeared because the deer have moved out.

On the other hand, if you understand that whitetails move to their winter ranges when snow reaches their knees, you can adjust your hunting pattern and put yourself where the deer are going to be.

In Maine, New Hampshire, and Vermont, where I do most of my deer hunting, deer commonly migrate from summer dispersal ranges where the population may be only six to 15 deer per square mile, into winter ranges that may harbor 100 to 200 deer per square mile. Unless you know where they go when they head for winter range, you would think there wasn't a deer left in the woods.

There is a distinct difference between winter range and a winter "deer yard." In northern parts of their range, whitetails commonly congregate for up to 12 weeks, depending on the weather, between January and March in traditional sheltered areas known as "deer yards." These yarding areas offer protection from wind and extreme cold temperatures, but may hold little forage of good nutritional quality.

The "winter range" is a much larger area, often adjacent to a deer yard, and is a center of activity during times when deer are not actually confined to the yards by extreme temperatures or deep snow. The winter range contains food sources (such as hanging moss and lichens, low-growing cedar, fir or hemlock browse, or hardwood tops dropped by logging operations) that remain available long after the lush summer foods are gone and snow has covered mast crops that have fallen to the ground.

The first knee-deep snow of the year motivates whitetails to move to their winter ranges on what may be a sort of reconnaissance patrol to assure themselves that a winter food source is still available there. Having reached the winter range, the deer often drift back out of it if the snow depth decreases, but will normally stay within a mile or so of the winter range, ready to move quickly back into it should heavy snow come again.

According to Gerry Lavigne, Maine's chief deer biologist, the depth of the snow is an impelling factor because foraging for food becomes less energy-efficient once deer can no longer lift their feet high enough to step over snow but must begin pushing through it with bent knees. A snowfall of ten inches reaches the knees of most deer, and gives them the impetus to start shifting their range.

Ten miles south of my cabin in northern New Hampshire is a major deer yard that attracts deer from as far as twenty miles away. The deer don't usually move into that yard until after Christmas, but a 10-inch snowfall in November is all it takes to start them streaming down out of their summer ranges toward the winter range surrounding that yard.

If we have six or eight inches of snow during deer season, tracks show that deer continue to move randomly from feeding to bedding areas without following any particular trail system. But let the snow reach ten inches, and everything changes.

Suddenly random movement stops and deer begin moving in parades, one behind the other, creating trails that quickly become hard-beaten paths — and most of the tracks will be pointed in the direction of the nearest winter range. Where one day you can find scattered deer tracks most anywhere, now you can move through the woods for a mile or more without crossing a track. Then you'll come upon several migratory trails in close proximity, where many deer passed in a short period of time.

These migratory trails normally follow major drainages; the sidehills above waterways may show the signs of heavy use, while other nearby hills become barren of all deer sign.

After years of observing the migratory routes that deer follow in my hunting territory, I have developed a pretty good idea of where I ought to be when a 10-inch snowfall comes. Several years ago I discovered a spot where three hardwood ridges come together and form a little bowl. Deer coming off these ridges during the migration period pass through the bowl. Their trails are not evident until the first deep snow comes, but then these deer highways get busy.

I went in there at dawn on the first deep snow last November and didn't cross the track of a single deer until I had completed the mile hike. When I reached the bowl, however, it looked like a sheep pasture with hard-packed trails intersecting where deer had poured through from the surrounding ridges. I scooped out a hole in the snow, propped some fir branches around me to break up my outline, and settled in, knowing I was in the right place.

It was only minutes before the first deer appeared. Two does, each trailed by a pair of offspring, passed through headed south, stepping high in the deepening snow. A few minutes later two more antlerless deer came in off one of the other ridges and drifted through the bowl. It was only a matter of time before a good buck was sure to come along, and soon he did, a nice 6-pointer that dressed out at 194 pounds.

When the migration begins, does and their offspring move out first. Adult bucks seem more reluctant to change their ways, and you will often find their tracks striding through the deepening snow, usually alone, crisscrossing the heavily used trails rather than traveling on them. Once they find sign of a doe in estrus, however, they go where the doe goes, so there is a general tendency for most bucks to follow the does toward the winter range.

Last to leave are the old bucks, many of whom have passed their peak years as breeders and are less compelled to follow the does. They often hang on in secret hiding places while the deepening snow protects them from any approaching hunters. Perhaps they will migrate to winter range later, perhaps they won't. If the snow gets chest deep and does not recede, these old bucks can be prevented from migrating and must face the hardships of winter under circumstances that can take a heavy toll.

Even in regions where deep snow does not usually last long and deer migrations are less pronounced, a shift from summer dispersal range to a more concentrated winter range still occurs. In the mid-Atlantic states, for example, deer move to steep, sunny hillsides when deep snow occurs. In flat country they move to heavy, protective cover. In all mountainous regions, deep snow at higher elevations drives them downhill into heavy cover.

The secret to hunting success is being able to put yourself in a place where a deer is about to appear. Knowing where deer go when deep snow comes to the country that you hunt can make the difference between seeing deer and just seeing tracks.

10

DEER HUNTING AS GOOD AS IT GETS

"**D**eer country doesn't get better than this!" Roy Knights declared as we topped a hill and viewed the landscape that stretched out before us. As far as we could see, steep hardwood-covered hills rose above softwood bottoms where careful forestry had produced strips of emerging new growth next to stands of protective older trees. A sparkling lake without a single cottage on its shoreline popped into view. Then the gravel road dropped down along the side of a dancing trout stream, later rising above a valley dammed by beavers. Deer tracks scuffed the road wherever we looked, and we kept seeing the ruffled lines of heavily used deer trails winding out through the woods.

We had entered Kenauk Reserve just north of Montibello, Quebec, which is about halfway between Montreal and Ottawa.

One of the longest-established private forest reserves in North America, Kenauk is also one of the largest privately owned reserves on the continent. No longer operating as a private club for wealthy members only, Kenauk Reserve is now managed for public hunting on a limited basis.

The reserve includes a 104-square-mile block of natural forest near the northern limit of whitetail range. Within its boundaries are ranks of jumbled mountains where red oak acorns and beechnuts litter the ground, more than seventy natural lakes, and many miles of free-flowing rivers and streams. Overlooking thirteen of the lakes are single isolated cabins that accommodate parties of four to twelve paying guests. Each cabin commands its own exclusive section of more than 2,000 acres of prime deer range.

Surveys indicate that the deer population in Kenauk averages 12 to 15 deer per square mile. Since wildlife species generally grow largest near the northern extremes of their natural range, Kenauk has a long-held reputation for producing BIG deer.

Each year hunters kill 60 to 70 deer in the reserve during Quebec's two-week mid-November season. The year before my visit, the Kenauk harvest included 54 bucks and nine does. Sixty-two percent of the bucks killed carried racks of six points or more, which matches the reserve's long-term average of about two-thirds of the bucks killed each year having six or more points, and 10 bucks (19 percent) dressed out at more than 200 pounds. The largest buck that year was a 13-pointer that dressed out at 230 pounds. An 11-pointer came in only a couple of pounds lighter, and the harvest included 25 large-bodied bucks with racks of eight and 10 points.

Roy Knights and I were driving into Kenauk, where we were going to meet two friends from Montreal and try to take advantage of this largely unknown hunting opportunity. We planned to spend five days hunting from a remote cabin with the ignominious name of Chalet Muskrat, a clean and comfortable four-bed abode overlooking a wide bay on the Kinonge River in the center of a typical Kenauk exclusive hunting zone.

We had just arrived at the chalet and hadn't even unpacked when Siegfried Gagnon spread a map on the table.

"Look at this territory!" he declared delightedly, his finger tracing our exclusive hunting zone. "We have a whole range of mountains, a couple of high mountain lakes with shoreline deer trails, miles of riverbank and a great big swamp to hunt, and nobody here but us. We all ought to have bucks on the pole by tomorrow night!"

Unlike more typical Kenauk hunters, the four of us are stillhunters. We planned to hunt separately, moving slowly through the woods, stopping here and there to watch and listen, hoping to see bucks before they saw, heard, or scented us.

"That's the best way to hunt here," Kenauk's recreational director, wildlife biologist Bill Nowell, had explained when we checked in. "Stillhunting is the way to get the big ones."

He explained that back when the Kenauk Reserve was used only by wealthy club members, it had become traditional to hire local men to conduct deer drives, with the shooters posted at likely crossings, waiting to shoot deer flushed by the drivers.

"That's the way it was always done here, and many of our hunters and guides still like to hunt that way. Trouble is, the older, bigger bucks have learned to avoid the drivers," he said.

We had arranged to use the services of two guides on the first two days in order to get acquainted with our territory. Michel and Daniel appeared at our cabin before daylight, eager to do a good job for us.

"We will put you at the major crossings, then we will do the dog and chase the deer to you," Michel insisted.

We announced that we preferred to stillhunt.

"That's okay for later," Michel said. "But first we must have a chase."

Reluctantly, we agreed to one drive. Might as well see how the guides like to do it, we said.

When I slipped in to the spot where I was to stand, I found two does already there. I settled silently against a tree and watched them pawing for acorns.

Half an hour later they were still feeding in plain sight, now not more than 40 yards away. Suddenly, both deers' heads went up, and they stared intently uphill. Far in the distance I heard the barking sounds of our drivers coming over the top of the mountain toward me.

The two deer stood listening. Then, as the barking sounds came closer, they switched their tails and began to move. But instead of moving away from the barking guides, they trotted uphill toward the oncoming drivers. As I watched, the two deer moved into a small thicket of evergreens and vanished. When the drivers came into view, the deer held their position, letting the two noisy drivers pass on either side of them. Once the drivers were below them, the deer came out into view again and began pawing for acorns once more. No deer were driven past any of our stands.

"No more barking," Siegfried ordered in French to our guides. "We just want you to show us some good places, and we will separate and hunt quietly alone."

With that straightened out, we began to hunt as we chose.

Carrying sandwiches, maps, and compasses, we spread out into the most remote regions of our huge territory. We each carried hand-held VHF radios and, for safety's sake as well as for company, we checked in with one another each hour on the hour. We spoke in whispers, telling each other where we were and what we were seeing.

"It's like a deer zoo here," Siegfried whispered at our first radio check. "I've never seen so much deer sign. I'm seeing does but no bucks yet. There are huge buck tracks everywhere and scrapes and rubs and big beds all over the place. It's only a matter of time."

Then Roy came on the air. "I can't talk now," he whispered in hushed tones. "I see a deer coming my way."

We never heard from our fourth member, Pierre, who was sneaking along a sidehill above the river. But a few minutes later there was a shot from his direction, and at our next radio check he had a happy report.

"My tag's filled," he said. "Six-pointer."

I ranged out across a mountain north of Lake Maholey and reached an area that was all tracked up by several uncommonly large bucks. Where three ravines came together and a maze of deer trails mingled, I found thirteen scrapes and more than a dozen antler rubs within a 100-yard area. Tracks and droppings and deer beds were everywhere.

"I've found the Mother Lode," I whispered at the next radio check. Then I settled back against a stump overlooking the area from the downwind side and waited there until it grew too dark to shoot. Two spike bucks and two groups of antlerless deer came by, but no big bucks showed.

The next day it began to snow. I was up on a mountaintop near a big trout lake where deer trails were so wide and rutted that they could have passed for bridle trails. I found a small cedar swamp that offered heavy cover and settled down in the snow to wait for a buck coming in, seeking shelter. Roy was on the other side of the same mountain, and Siegfried was west of us on a hill overlooking the lake.

After about an hour I saw a good-looking buck cross an opening, headed my way, but he disappeared into the heavy cover and never showed up at my end of the swamp. I circled out until I picked up his track and followed him, hoping that he had bedded and that the falling snow would cover my approach. Two hours later, more than a mile from where I had taken the track, and far out on the mountainside amidst rugged granite ledges, I knew that I was catching up with him.

The snow had grown shin-deep and the falling flakes swirled, making it difficult to see clearly far ahead, but the buck's track was very fresh in the drifting snow.

I had just rounded an outcropping of ledge and was moving through open hardwood timber above a little brook when I saw the buck moving below me a bit less than 100 yards away. As he turned broadside to cross the brook, I yanked the cover off my Leupold 2–1/2 to 8×variable scope, screwed it up to 4 power, and brought my Remington .280 to bear.

My single shot was muffled by the falling snow and nobody heard it. Later, when I announced on the radio that I was moving downhill to the west dragging a fat 6-pointer and didn't know where I'd come out, Roy's voice came back. "What did you do, find a dead one? I never heard you shoot."

The skies were gray the day after the snowstorm, and deer were on the move everywhere. By noon Roy had tagged a nice 8-pointer that he had shot through the neck as it lay in its bed.

"I could move quietly in the snow," he explained. "He never knew I was there." Roy had spotted the bedded buck before it detected him, mounted his rifle carefully, and made a perfect kill. That left only Siegfried to trudge the snowclad hills alone.

"Does, does, and more does," he mournfully reported by radio. "Why can't I see horns?"

His shot came the fourth morning when a nice 6-pointer moved out from under a thick stand of dark fir trees close to the river, 75 yards ahead of him. The buck turned to look back, and Siegfried found his shoulder in the scope.

On our last morning, when we all had our deer loaded and were almost ready to leave, Bill Nowell stopped to tell us that Tony

Merlo, a hunter in another Kenauk cabin a few miles away, had killed a very large buck and was asking for help getting it out of the woods.

Merlo, who's from Montreal, is an older man whose health limits his ability to get around in the mountains. During his stay in camp he had already missed two bucks and was so discouraged that the previous afternoon he had told his hunting partner, Werner Sapp, that he didn't want to hunt any more.

But Werner, who already had a good buck hanging up, had seen the track of a very big deer crossing a little swamp not far from a logging road. He convinced Tony to go there at 3 P.M. and stay until dark.

"He just sat down, and ten minutes later he shot this thing," Werner told us, pointing to the great buck that lay in the snow. The deer was a wide-racked 11-pointer that dressed out at 228 pounds.

"I found a good place to sit near the edge of the swamp and got settled and right away I saw him coming through the woods toward me," Tony said. "The first thing I saw was his rack, then I saw the deer. He was huge."

Before the deer even reached the edge of the forest, Tony took careful aim and dropped the big buck in its tracks with a single shot at more than 100 yards.

"He could have waited and let the deer come closer," Werner chuckled. "The deer was coming toward him when he fired.

"You're lucky you didn't miss this one, too," Werner told Tony. "Your heart couldn't have stood that."

"My heart never felt better," Tony replied as the rest of us dragged his enormous buck out of the woods.

11

HOW TO HAVE MORE BIG BUCKS

Want to see more trophy bucks in your state's deer population? It can be done. In fact, the state of Maine has increased the number of trophy bucks in its annual harvest without limiting hunters from taking smaller bucks if they wish.

Over the past 12 years, Maine's Department of Inland Fisheries and Wildlife has restructured the deer population so that its recent all-time record-setting annual buck harvests are more than 50 percent higher than they were when the management program began. Even more impressive, almost one out of four bucks now killed in Maine is a trophy 4–1/2- to 5–1/2-year-old animal that has attained maximum weight and antler size. Overall, 61 percent of the bucks now being killed in Maine are older than 2–1/2 and have developed antler racks and body size that satisfy most hunters.

Maine's total wintering deer population has been rebuilt from 160,000 in the early 1980s to more than 255,000 today, and the hunter-success rate has climbed substantially. Only a few years ago fewer than one out of eight Maine hunters tagged a deer; by 1997 more than one out of six were successful.

How did they do it?

Maine uses a simple and inexpensive system to assess the deer habitat potential in each of its 30 separate deer management zones. Then it manipulates the population levels in each zone by carefully regulating how many adult does hunters kill there.

"We actually let the deer tell us where they are getting over-crowded and need thinning, and where habitat exists that can support more deer," says Maine's deer biologist Gerry Lavigne. "By examining deer killed in each management zone, we determine the well-being of the deer population in whatever zone they came from."

Each hunting season, Maine's biologists make daily checks at meat processing plants, deer registration stations, and highway check stations to examine 1–1/2-year-old bucks as they are brought in from various deer management zones (1–1/2-year-old bucks are easily identified because their premolar teeth are newly erupted at that age).

"Deer are what they eat," Lavigne notes. "In young bucks, body growth takes precedence over antler growth. Poorly nourished bucks produce stunted antlers. If the average antler diameter on 1–1/2-year-old bucks brought in from a certain zone is below normal, it indicates that deer in that zone were undernourished last year and that we need to reduce the deer population there. We accomplish that by issuing more Any-Deer permits for that area the following year, to encourage more hunters to kill antlerless deer in that zone. In zones where the average antler diameter is larger than normal, we know that deer have not yet reached their optimum population level. We

can encourage the deer population to continue increasing by not issuing Any-Deer permits in those zones. Wherever average antler diameter is normal, it tells us to preserve the status quo by holding the
deer population at current numbers."

Fawns and adult does killed by hunters are also examined for
indications of herd health in each management zone. Where fawn
body weights are average or higher, biologists can expect that the
food supply is adequate or abundant and that those zones can support more deer. Checking for milk in the udders of adult does re-
veals if they have successfully reared fawns that year or lost them.
This gives biologists important information on whether or not deer
populations in each zone are replacing deer killed by hunters,
predators, vehicles, and other means. As long as there is evidence
that does are successfully rearing more fawns than adults are being
lost, the herd grows.

Maine's goal is to maintain the deer population at about half
the maximum number of animals the habitat in each zone can support in winter. Statewide, that adds up to about 300,000 wintering
deer, or 10 deer per square mile. That leaves a wide margin of available habitat as insurance against the catastrophic die-offs that can
occur on an overcrowded range during a severe winter. At 50 percent of the maximum sustainable deer population level, relatively
high hunter harvests can be expected, the deer population remains
productive, deer are available for viewing by nonhunters, and the
potential for deer/people conflicts is considered acceptable.

Each year some 90,000 hunters (about half of Maine's total
number of hunters) apply for anywhere from 24,000 to 55,000 Any-
Deer permits, depending on year-by-year deer population conditions. Since 1986, when the state's first Any-Deer permits were issued, Maine has refined its ability to achieve an adult doe harvest
that is predictably within five percent of its desired quota, despite
the fact that holders of Any-Deer permits are not limited to taking

adult does. (Statistics prove that for each six Any-Deer permits that are issued, one adult doe will be harvested.)

By restricting adult doe harvests to desired quotas in zones where deer populations are high and stimulating population growth by limiting the doe harvest in zones where optimum deer numbers have not yet been attained, Maine has restructured its doe herd to contain a higher percentage of older, more successful breeders. As the population expands, an equal number of fawns of both sexes are added. This results in a higher antlered buck population two years down the road.

As the number of bucks in the herd increases, the number of bucks that survive to maturity also increases.

"The key to having more big bucks is reducing hunting pressure on bucks of all ages," Lavigne declares. "The more hunting pressure you focus on bucks, the fewer big bucks you'll have."

12

THE REWARDS OF RATTLING

The only way I like to hunt deer is in solitude. I don't want to shoot a deer off a drive or even a deer that comes past because somebody else stirred him up. I search out places where deer are undisturbed and moving naturally. I like to think that getting a buck is more a matter of skill than of fate.

That is why I am intrigued with the concept of luring a buck into gun range by rattling antlers and creating the sounds of two bucks fighting. Rattling adds an extra element of skill to deer hunting, increasing the challenge and sweetening the reward when it works.

The technique has been publicized in Texas so much that some hunters could get the idea that antler rattling only works in the mesquite brush and desert country. On the contrary, the technique will attract bucks wherever the deer population is thick enough to make bucks compete for does. In the breeding season bucks must use every one of their senses to locate does during the brief periods that they are in estrus. The buck's powers of scent, sight, and hearing are finely tuned to pick up signals of an estrus doe's whereabouts. At this time, he's highly responsive to any sound that triggers the idea that an unbred doe is close by.

If you think antler rattling is just something Texans do, you ought to meet my friend Normand LeBrasseur. He's a hunting guide on whitetail-rich Anticosti Island, off the coast of Quebec. Norman didn't learn antler rattling from a Texan, I'll vouch for that. He learned to rattle from his grandfather in French Canada, where antler rattling has been a traditional method for attracting big bucks since before colonization.

"My gran'father learned rattling from Indians," Normand told me. "They would get bucks that way with bows and arrows in the old time." When you think about that, there is every reason to believe that antler rattling would have been a logical method for bow-and-arrow–armed Indians to use to bring deer in close. And Indians would have practiced rattling, just as they knew how to attract waterfowl within arrow or sling range by jerking a fox skin back and forth across a beach in view of geese or ducks rafted on open water. Rattling was undoubtedly a technique used by Indians the length and breadth of deer range. It is from them that Texans probably learned it, too.

I went rattling on Anticosti Island one November, near the end of the season. We stayed at the comfortable and rustic Bell River Lodge, operated by Anticosti Outfitters. There, at the eastern end of the island, where deer hunting access has only been opened up in the past few years, the number of big bucks is high, and 8-point racks are the average. With a limit of two deer per hunter and guarantees

DEER WOODS DIARY

Here's Jim coming back to camp with the 10-pointer he killed on the last day of our Minnesota canoe/camping trip. Jim made his shot so far back in the woods that he dragged the buck all day and never reached the river. Next morning he finished the drag, got the buck in his canoe and headed back to camp.

Bucks like this are usually nocturnal. They don't move much in daylight until the rut. Then they sometimes lose their sense of caution and reveal themselves. This Maine 11-pointer has his mind on a doe he's following out of his safety zone.

New Hampshire stillhunter Alfred Balch whittles a stick the width of the largest buck track he finds and uses it to identify the same buck's track when he finds it elsewhere. He says, "If the deer aren't moving, the hunter has to move, or there's not going to be an encounter."

We use canoes to gain access to deer country that is hard to reach from roads. When you separate yourself from other hunters, you find whitetails that are behaving according to their natural inclinations.

Where hunting pressure is heavy, deer often leave the open woods to spend daylight hours hidden in high grass swamps such as this. If hunters approach, the deer merely move out of sight and bed down again.

Good maps of your hunting territory are essential. Jim made this book, which combines topographic maps and aerial photos of an area we sometimes hunt in Maine's Allagash region.

When a buck comes in to rattling antlers, he expects to see two bucks in battle. He expects to see movement.

Wyoming cowboys told us we'd need 4-wheel-drive trucks and horses to reach deer country, but we found plenty of bucks on public land by floating the Big Horn River. The deer spend their days close to the river, and then move out to feed on private ranchlands at night.

On canoe/hunting trips, we usually carry two wall tents; one for cooking, the other for sleeping. The cook tent is equipped with a propane cook-stove and lanterns, and we use a woodstove for heat. We build a dining table out of logs and plywood and bring along folding chairs. A meatpole can also come in handy.

This is the section of the Missouri River in Montana where Lewis and Clark found deer most abundant in 1805. It's mostly public land today. We canoed in, set up a tent camp, and found whitetails plentiful in the brush along the river and mule deer in the high country.

We used horses to reach a remote section of Anticosti Island in Quebec and found bucks like this that had rarely, if ever, encountered man before. We each tagged two good bucks in a few days. I've never seen a place where deer came more readily to rattling antlers and grunt calls.

Here's an 8-pointer I encountered while stillhunting from our tent camp up on the St. John River in Maine. I'd seen a doe pass and waited. Ten minutes later this buck came along, following her track.

We made birchbark horns and called for moose along the Pivabiska River in northern Ontario. To reach this place we paddled 40 miles north from the last road. Later, with canoes laden with moose meat, we paddled more than 100 miles to reach a railroad, where we loaded the moose and canoes onto a freight train and headed home.

Jim and Dean approaching the moose Jim shot with a muzzleloader up on the Pivabiska. We waded in up to our thighs to dress the moose out. You can't drag one of these critters.

To this Inuit boy, a caribou's hind leg tendon is like bubble gum. He can slice off a chunk with his knife and chew it all day. He's settled down with a good supply.

A caribou family in September on the Leaf River in Quebec; grandfather, father, mother, and son. Note the regal effect of Grandpa's peeling velvet. These are actually only average antlers in the Leaf River herd.

When we were hunting caribou with the Crees, Sam Tapiatic's snowmobile broke through the frozen crust of a remote lake and sank into slush. We hurriedly dragged spruce boughs to make a dry bed and managed to pull the machine out, clear the slush from the dolly wheels before they froze, and continue the hunt.

Here's what trophy hunters are looking for; a wide, double-shoveled rack with palmated antlers and lots of points. This caribou has just shed his velvet, leaving his antlers red with blood. I shot him with my camera but did not raise my rifle. Hunting with Inuits has taught me to save my tags for the tender meat of barren female caribou.

Harry Baxter uses a canoe to reach elk country that is not accessible to vehicles. Harry paddles into pockets of unhunted country, sets up a camp and goes after elk on foot. The year I joined him, Harry came out with a nice one, true to form.

There's always a heavily traveled deer trail in the alders close to riverbanks and lakeshores. I've connected with a lot of good bucks in low country just like this.

Bucks like this are why I built my log cabin exactly where it is.

This is my cabin on the New Hampshire–Quebec border. It's in country rich in deer, moose, bear, grouse, and woodcock, and there are trout in the swimming hole out front. Much of this book was written right here.

that each pair of hunters will have several square miles of hunting territory each day, it is my kind of place.

"Now is the best time for rattling," Normand told me. "Many females are bred by now. They are hiding from the bucks. The bucks are looking all the time for one that doesn't run away."

I had brought along a pair of synthetic antlers manufactured by Johnny Stewart, Inc. of Waco, Texas. I'd been given lessons in using them by Johnny Stewart himself and had seen the plastic rack bring in 13 big whitetail bucks in just three days down on the sprawling Tomas Ranch in south Texas.

Normand didn't like them.

"No good," he said. "Plastic."

He had a set of the real things, with the brow tines sawed off so they wouldn't spike his hands when he bashed the antlers together. I pointed out that the Johnny Stewart antlers had no brow tines to begin with and had extra-long main beams so that the rattler's hands were safely separated when the rattling was done, but Normand was having none of it. The first morning he left my antlers in the lodge kitchen, behind a box under the stove in the waitresses' room "by accident." So, we used his horns and they worked fine.

"Good noise," Normand said, demonstrating his rattling technique.

I could only agree. He bashed the antlers together, then twisted them to make the tines interlock and rattle. He kept it up for about a minute, then pulled the antlers apart with a twisting motion that sounded just like what it was, antlers separating under tension. Then he pawed the earth with one antler, stamped it into the ground, and used it to knock against a tree root and break twigs around him. Had you been a buck within hearing range, you could not mistake the sounds for anything but those of a buck fight, and if your neck were swollen with the rut and you were obsessed with the mad desire to mate, the sounds would fire your brain with the jealous suggestion that the combatants had located a hot doe. You would respond at a trot, throwing caution to the wind as all true suitors must, and let your passion drive you on.

That is exactly how the bucks behaved. One of the first things you find out when you start rattling for bucks is that you had better be ready. If there is a lonesome buck within 300 yards of you when you begin to rattle, chances are he'll show himself within a minute. If he's farther away, your rattling may not be heard, depending on wind and terrain.

On that first day with Normand, we crept quietly to the edge of a section of forest that had been toppled by a windstorm some years earlier and had grown back in high grass and short spruces. It was just the kind of place that deer retire to in midday, and we picked places to sit about 30 yards apart in hopes that a buck sneaking toward Normand's rattling would present a clear shot for me or my hunting partner, Al Diem.

Normand bashed and gnashed his antlers, raked them through branches, stomped them into the earth with pawing motions, and generally raised hell. When he was about 60 seconds into his act, I saw a deer moving off to my right, about 100 yards away. It proved to be a spike traveling with a pair of does. They watched and listened for a few moments, then disappeared into the bush, circling to get downwind of us.

Then Normand stopped rattling and was silent for a couple of minutes; then he began a second stanza. Suddenly, I saw him duck his head and peer through the spruce branches that surrounded him. It was clear from his attitude that he had a deer in view. From my angle, I couldn't see a thing. Then Normand looked at me and nodded. He held his rattling antlers up beside his head and pointed with a finger, indicating that he could see a buck. Then he rattled some more, trying to make the buck take the few steps that would bring him into my view, but the buck held, studying the spot where the sounds were coming from.

Normand gestured for me to to slip forward, to stalk the immobile deer. I rose and started to sneak across the needle-carpeted forest floor. As I stepped past the edge of a thick spruce clump, the buck, an 8-pointer, saw me and leapt in a high arc over a fallen log. This time I was ready, and when the butt of the little custom-fitted Remington mountain rifle hit my shoulder, the picture in the Leupold sight was all deer; I simply slid the crosshairs behind the buck's shoulder and squeezed off the shot as he dashed through an opening not 30 yards away.

That's the easy way to do it, having one man rattle while wingmen wait for the shot. Hunting alone is different, as I discovered in the days that followed.

To Normand's dismay, I insisted that he return my synthetic antlers and let me rattle up a second deer on my own. I had seen the plastic antlers repeatedly bring in deer in Texas, and I did not share Normand's distrust of them. To my ear, they made a very real sound, only louder.

The next day Norman went off with Al while I went into the woods alone and began learning about the flip side of rattling.

I knew the procedure. I hunted into the wind, moving slowly and silently, staying in the shadows and not exposing myself in front of backlit clearings. When I came to one of those extra-thick patches of forest where you just know deer hide during the day, I picked out a place in the shadows and crept to it making no disturbance.

A soft wind was blowing in my face, straight from the thicket to me. The timber between me and the thick place was open enough so that I could get a clear shot if a buck came out and approached me. I thought I was ready.

I began by loudly raking the brush around me and then slammed the antlers together with a whack that could be heard for several hundred yards. Then I moderated the sound, twisting the antlers together and clicking the tines. Deer fights are push and shove affairs, with head-twisting movements causing the antlers to rattle and grind. I kept it up for about 45 seconds, then broke off sharply. A moment later I bumped one antler against a tree four or five times, then thudded it into the earth and pawed loudly. I paused for a few moments, then began another 45-second rattling routine.

Ten minutes later, I was ready to move on. I had seen no movement in front of me and no indication that any deer had heard my efforts. I waited a moment more, then stuck the antlers in my belt, picked up my rifle, and stood up.

As I rose, there was a crashing rush behind me and I spun to see a heavily antlered buck burst through the brush and dash into the heaviest cover. He gave me no shot.

Right behind me, not more than 30 yards away and straight downwind! He had come in silently, stalking the sounds until he was close enough to see me and smell me. Yet he hadn't fled until I stood up.

That told me something. That buck was so sure that my rattling was made by two bucks fighting that he had come all the way in, despite the warnings that his nose and eyes must have given him. He had smelled me and not run off. He had seen me crouched there rattling and had not believed what his nose and eyes were telling him. Fully in the rut and so eager to breed that he was blind to caution, that buck came in without hesitation. That's how badly he wanted me to be two bucks fighting over a doe in estrus.

I had blown my chance for a shot by not expecting the buck to approach from downwind. I would not make that mistake again.

By the end of that day, I had rattled in five bucks. Three of them had antlers that I would have been proud to hang on the wall, while the other two were forkhorns. During the day I had also seen half a dozen does slink off with their heads down and their ears back when I began rattling, but two had approached me. I figured those that left were probably already bred or not in estrus, and that the two that showed interest in the sounds and came in were not yet bred.

That was one of the most frustrating days of my hunting career. The rattling worked so well that there was no excuse for me coming back empty-handed, yet I had fired only one shot all day, and that one missed.

One buck appeared within a few seconds after I went to work with the antlers. He showed about 150 yards out, trotting through an opening with his big rack rocking from side to side. Then he got behind some blowdowns and came straight at me, his eyes riveted on my position. I was crouched down, my rifle leaning against a tree within easy reach. I waited for him to disappear behind something so I could grab my rifle, but he just kept coming, walking now, ears cocked forward and eyes seeming to look straight into mine. I was paralyzed by his stare, unable to reach for my rifle without being seen.

At 35 yards he stopped beside a short fir tree and peered at me from around its edge. It was now or never. I slowly reached for the rifle, but my hand had only just begun to move when the buck gave a snort, drew his head back behind the cover of the tree, and bounded into the thick stuff, leaving me shaken and feeling foolish.

At another spot, I had rattled for perhaps two minutes when a buck suddenly appeared. This time my rifle was ready, laid out across a log in front of me where I could pick it up without having to reach for it, and screened behind a bit of brush so I could shoulder it unnoticed. I was in a clump of firs at the edge of a big open heath, facing into the wind and the forest. No deer could slip around behind me this time, and I would be able to shoulder my rifle without being seen if one should appear in front of me.

Again it was a big buck that suddenly drifted into view about 100 yards back in the forest. I rattled passionately for a moment more and then, when the buck walked behind by a nearby tree, I laid down the horns and took up my rifle, nestling the butt into my shoulder and settling back against a stump. The buck had not reappeared on the other side of the tree that hid him, so I knew he was either standing there waiting or coming toward me behind the cover of the tree.

The next thing I saw was an eyeball shining through the tangled branches of a blowdown about 40 yards away. It stared, unblinking, precisely at the spot where I sat hidden. I could make out a dark, stained antler soaring out above the shining eyeball, but I could see nothing of the rest of the deer.

He had slipped within 40 yards by using that tree for cover, then came up behind the blowdown, keeping his body screened from my view all the way, and now he was right there eyeballing me. I thumbed the scope up to full 8 × magnification, making that eyeball gleam like a Christmas tree ornament.

Should I try it? Or would he take the single step that would put his whole head in view? I've killed deer with head shots, but the *eyeball?* The idea was somehow messy and distasteful. I wanted that white patch on the neck—a shot where the neck meets the shoulder, something solid. But all I had was an eyeball, and it was close!

So, I squeezed off the shot and sent a .280-caliber, 165-grain soft-point bullet directly through the space between the eye and the antler of a deer that stood in such a way that the space was simply space, and the bullet flew through it and stopped in a tree many yards out. The buck was gone before I could jack in another round.

After that I had some time to fool around with smaller deer that I didn't want to shoot and, of course, they pranced around in full view, stood broadside at 30 yards, even came back after I showed myself, shooed them away, and then sat down and rattled again.

I had a little forkhorn so totally awed by my sounds that he wouldn't run off even when I rose up. He just stood staring at me, trying to make me look like a deer.

Late in the afternoon I rattled in the day's third big buck. Normand had told me there was a sly old buck that hung out around a swamp so thick that hunters could not move into it without making sounds and alerting the buck.

"Go in there and stay in one place," he advised. "Sit for a long time before you rattle. Then stay there in the same place and rattle every 15 minutes or so. When the buck moves into hearing range, he may come to you."

I found the place and saw that the area was tracked up with big splayed hoofprints. I passed half a dozen scrapes and rubbed trees. This was a big buck's hangout, all right. I settled in beside a stump at the edge of the swamp, waited a while, then went to work. There was no wind, and I was sure my rattling sounds could be heard a long way off. I would rattle on and off for 10 minutes or so, then wait 15 minutes and start again. I pictured the big buck patrolling his swamp, and willed him to come into hearing range.

I never did see him coming. He must have come in behind the screen of trees, tiptoeing and staying hidden all the way—as the big ones often do. I didn't know he was there until he snorted. The snort seemed close and loud, and I scrutinized the thickets and blowdowns, but I couldn't find him. Snorter and snortee were locked in a mutual search for one another, and neither of us could make out the other.

I reached for the plastic antlers and once more began conducting a symphony of deer fight overtures. But as the horns clacked and rattled, a cold draft came up and assailed me from behind. The late afternoon breeze was blowing in the worst possible direction, directly from me to the buck.

This deer was no young sprout so eager to see a deer fight that man scent didn't register. This was an old one who was far past the age of lustful abandon. He put his safety first, and with the first whiff of me he was off and away, with his white flag clamped down tight and his heavy rack obscured by the thick growth. I got a glimpse, enough to know he was the best one yet, but I could only listen to him crash away and wish I'd seen him sooner.

That's the way deer rattling goes. Getting a buck to respond is only part of it. Being in a position to shoot accurately when a shot presents itself is equally important. You must select a place to rattle from that gives you good visibility, yet allows you to remain hidden. Your rifle must be placed where it is instantly at hand and can be mounted without the movement being seen. The wind, if there is any, should be blowing in your face from the direction in which you expect the deer to appear—but don't forget to watch the downwind side, too.

There's a lot that can go wrong when you are rattling for bucks, but when it works you remember the special satisfaction for a long, long time.

My first complete success came the next morning, without warning. I had just hit the track of a good buck crossing a hardwood knob and started to follow it when I saw the brightness of an open swamp up ahead through the trees. Does often hang around swamp edges, and I figured the buck might be right there, watching and waiting for a doe.

I crawled in behind a log that gave me cover, rested my rifle close at hand, and took the antlers from my belt. Because I had a gut feeling that the buck might be close, I opened with a soft ticking of antler tips, rather than a loud bashing. Then I used the horns to scrape the ground, making pawing sounds, then a moment later brushed the antlers together again, only harder this time.

I had only just begun to twist and grind the horns together when I saw a flicker of movement near the swamp edge. I kept on rattling, gradually increasing the tempo and level of aggression, finally bashing the back sides of the main beams together in an awful smack that resounded through the forest. Then I ground the antlers together, twisted them against one another, then separated them by pulling them apart with the pressure still applied, making a zinging sound.

When I laid the antlers aside, I heard a twig snap on my right. I brought the rifle up in front of me and got ready. Then there was a rush of hooves and I saw the buck bound across an opening and disappear into a fringe of spruce and fir. I slowly turned to face that direction, brought my rifle butt to my shoulder, and waited. Then I caught movement back toward the swamp and focused on that long enough to see that a doe was coming toward me.

When I turned my eyes back to the place where the buck had disappeared, he was right there. His wide 8-point rack stuck out past his ears, and the tines rose above his head in a graceful basket shape. The front half of his body was outside the cover, and I simply slid the crosshairs behind his shoulder, thumbed off the safety, and squeezed the trigger.

Since that memorable day, I have rarely hunted deer during the rut without using rattling antlers. In the intervening years they have brought numerous bucks to both my gun and my camera, and have added a whole extra element of satisfaction to deer hunting.

What has impressed me most is how quickly bucks respond to rattling. If one hears you and is going to come, he's going to come right now. I generally expect to see a deer move within two minutes of the beginning of a rattling session if one is going to come. Sometimes the reaction is almost immediate. If a deer has not appeared within five minutes, I don't expect to see one. If I haven't seen one after waiting 15 minutes, I usually move on.

Deer generally show far out first, then either circle to get downwind or come in behind cover that screens their approach. Be ready to respond at any moment. It is surprising how many times they appear before you expect them too, before you are ready.

Rattling works anywhere, but it works most often in areas where the deer population is heavy and balanced enough to make competition for does commonplace. Furthermore, you have to be rattling within hearing distance of a buck that is looking for action. Bucks that have fought other bucks for the attentions of a doe will recognize the sounds and will usually respond to them during the breeding season, unless they are already in the company of a doe.

Rattling is not as effective before the rut. However, bucks will come to the sounds of rattling antlers long after the peak of breeding season has passed. They are hoping to find a doe that did not conceive during the rut, and will keep looking for such does right up until their antlers drop.

Bucks become increasingly cautious where rattling is popular among hunters. Once they've been duped and found that the sounds were made by a man, and not by two bucks fighting, they will be harder to fool next time. Rattling is most effective, therefore, where deer populations are high and few other hunters use the rattling technique.

Even in areas where deer populations are sparse, rattling is worth trying during and after the rut. When you're following the track of a buck that leads into a thick place, try settling outside the thicket and rattling instead of following the tracks into the thick stuff. When you're close to a place where the buck may be resting, rattling will often draw him out.

I'm convinced that synthetic antlers work as well as real ones, and they are certainly more comfortable to use and carry. Furthermore, the best sounds are made by heavy antlers; and how many hunters want to saw up a trophy rack to use for rattling when good synthetic ones are available?

The most gratifying thing about rattling is the knowledge that you are doing something that may make a deer appear, as opposed to just wandering around in the woods hoping to see one. Rattling is not a precise science. There's no singular best way to rattle. The fun is in making up the performance as you go along, creating the sounds of a buck fight that you can picture in your mind. Thumps, grunts, breaking brush, pawing the ground, and knocking against trees are as much a part of your performance as the rattling itself.

It all adds an element of skill and anticipation to the hunt, one that makes the whole experience more satisfying.

13

TALK
LIKE A
DEER

With a misty rain making the woods dank and silent, I left the road and struck north along a little brook. I hunted in wide loops, circling out to the side and then back to the brook valley, moving slowly and stopping often to wait and watch. The only sounds were the raindrops dripping from the trees and the occasional rasping croak of a soggy raven complaining about the weather.

Deer sign increased as I got farther from the road. Droppings littered the ground in pockets where deer had browsed striped maple twigs. When I came upon a fresh scrape I knelt and examined it, noting the large track a buck had left stamped into the damp soil.

"Do you ever call deer?" Jean Gagnon had asked me as we drove out that morning to my hunting zone.

"Never tried," I answered.

He pulled out a little plastic call about the size of a jackknife. It was simply two flat pieces of plastic held together with a pair of elastic bands, but when he put it to his lips and gently blew through it the sound that came out was a soft but resonant "aaannh."

It was not loud, but the call had a low-level frequency that would carry well in wet, silent woods. I figured I could have heard it 100 yards away, even with my "shotgun ears." The call would be audible to a deer at much greater distance.

"Take this with you and try making just one or maybe two soft calls like that whenever you stop and sit for a while," Jean said. "When you accidentally snap a twig, use the call to blame the sound on a deer.

"When a doe is in heat she bleats like that from time to time," Jean explained. "A doe comes in heat for less than 24 hours at a time only once every three weeks. That means when she's ready a buck has to find her in a hurry. Bucks are listening for this sound and when they hear it, they respond to it."

He said that his clients at Bell River Lodge had been using doe bleat calls and were convinced they were effective.

So now, looking at the buck track in the scrape, I pulled the call out of my pocket and considered it. I figured it wouldn't hurt to make a call. The sound would not scare a buck away, yet it might attract one that was back in the thick growth.

I placed the call to my lips and blew softly, trying to make my breath as even as possible from start to finish. I made the sound last for about a second, then waited half a minute and called once more. Then I put the call away and waited.

A whiskeyjack fluttered in the spruce above my head, and the sudden sound jarred my nerves. In the quiet woods even the soft fluttering of a bird sounded loud. Certainly, my call had been heard farther away than I could see.

"Remember where you made calls and be especially careful as you approach those places on your way back out of the woods," Jean had advised. "Sometimes you'll find a buck has come to your call after you left and is waiting there when you come back."

My first call produced no response, but it felt good to have made an attempt. The sound had been natural and non-alarming, and it pleased me to be doing more than just sneaking around looking for deer. Calling, I found, adds a new sensation of anticipation to deer hunting.

I called in several places that morning. I called whenever I found a scrape with a large, fresh buck track in it. I figured that if a doe in heat encountered such evidence of a buck's whereabouts, she might choose that moment to make her presence known. The call was so soft and non-disruptive that I was confident it did no harm, and there was a chance it might produce the sight of a buck.

I can't say the big buck I shot that morning was definitely responding to my call, but then neither can I be sure he was not. It happened like this:

I had made a call at the site of a scrape and had waited fifteen minutes or so, then moved on when nothing showed. Coming upon a tangle of fallen spruce trees, I was picking my way through the upright branches and climbing over the fallen trunks and was just coming out of the worst of it when I spotted a slight movement in my peripheral vision. I froze. Sure enough, in the center of a thicket of young Christmas tree-sized fir trees, one of the little firs was thrusting back and forth as if someone was shaking it.

I eased up against a dark stump to break my outline and watched. The little tree stopped moving briefly, then started thrashing more violently than before. I couldn't see what was causing the commotion, but I was beginning to feel certain that the little tree was being hooked by an antlered buck whose body was hidden by the surrounding clump of firs.

I left my stump and took a few careful steps along the mossy brookside deer trail, keeping my eyes on the moving tree. There was no wind. The air stood still and I was able to creep silently through the wet, silent woods until I was within 50 yards. Coming upon a hump of moss-covered ground, I stepped up on it; from that level I could clearly see the shape of a broad brown back within the firs.

I shouldered my rifle and checked the hairy back through the scope. It was a deer, that was sure, but I couldn't see its head or any sign of antlers. The deer changed position, and now I could see its entire shoulder and midsection. I dropped the crosshairs to a spot low behind the shoulder and could almost see the beating of the deer's heart, yet still no antlers showed. The body was large and husky, the shoulder heavy. It was a buck, I was sure, but I kept the safety on and waited.

Finally, the buck raised its head, and even though I still could not see its face, the wide brown antlers jutted out on either side of the little fir. I couldn't see enough to count points, but the sheer width of the rack made it clear that this was a better than average buck.

"Good enough," I whispered to myself, then slid the crosshairs back behind his shoulder and dropped him.

The buck proved to be an 8-pointer with a handsome 22-inch rack.

Now I can't say for sure that he was coming to my call. Yet I had called just minutes before from a scrape less than 100 yards from where I had found him. He was clearly close enough to have heard the call on that wet, quiet morning. Was that thrashing fir tree a signal meant to attract the doe he thought had made the call? The tree he was thrashing proved not to be rubbed. The buck had merely tangled his antlers in the lower branches and tossed it back and forth in a flagging motion.

That night I repeated the episode to head guide Jean-Marc Levesque as we hung my buck in the meat shed.

"Yes, I think he was signaling the doe," Jean-Marc said. "Bucks sometimes come close when you make a call, but stay hidden and call the doe to them.

"Did he tap his hoof?" Jean-Marc asked.

To tell the truth, I didn't know. I couldn't remember hearing any sound at all.

"That's the other thing they do to call a doe," he said. "They tap their hoof against a root in a special way that means, 'I'm here.'"

Next morning Jean-Marc showed me what he meant. He had come along to show me a remote area way off the road, where three brooks converged in a big swampy area. Sharing my belief that big bucks often travel near water, Jean-Marc agreed that big bucks would like a place like that.

On the way in through the woods, we jumped a doe from her bed in a thick place where wind had toppled a group of trees. She bounded off into the forest, blowing loud alarm calls and warning every deer within earshot that danger was approaching.

"Watch this," Jean-Marc whispered. He dropped to his knees and whipped out his jackknife. Now he tapped the knife handle against a protruding root five times in an even cadence, about one tap every half-second. Five times he tapped, then paused. Then five times again.

"Always five taps," he whispered.

He stayed crouched low and out of sight next to a thick tree trunk, with me crouching right beside him. Every so often he'd peek out around the edge of the tree, then tap again. After a couple of minutes he peeked again, then winked at me.

"She's coming back," he whispered.

I peeked and, sure enough, here came the doe. Behind her followed two more antlerless deer. When Jean-Marc tapped, their ears would prick up and waggle; then they would take a few more steps in our direction with their necks outstretched, big eyes luminous and wet black noses sniffing the air currents. They moved closer each time Jean-Marc tapped, until the lead doe was standing no more than ten yards from us. All three were studying the spot were we crouched concealed.

"This is how the buck calls his doe to him," he said. "He taps his hoof on a root five times. Always five times. It's a signal. Sometimes they tap and sometimes they thrash a bush, like your buck did, to tell the doe where they are when there's no wind to carry their scent. Your buck may have been tapping, too, and you didn't hear it or didn't know what the sound was."

Maybe so.

When we came to the three forks that Jean-Marc had described, the place was well marked with buck sign. Several big scrapes and half a dozen rubbed trees told us that this was a place where several buck territories overlapped. We stopped in the shadows and made a couple of soft doe bleats, then waited. When nothing had appeared after 15 minutes, we moved on.

After an hour or so the air began to move and it became useless to go farther in the direction we had been traveling, for the wind was now on our backs. We made a wide circle, then began hunting into the wind.

Late in the morning we were coming down the valley of one of the three brooks towards the confluence. Jean-Marc stopped me and whispered, "Just ahead is where we called. Be extra careful here."

I moved as quietly as possible, staying in the shadows and stopping beside thick tree trunks. Up ahead I could see the wider opening where the three brooks joined. I could just make out the log we had sat on when Jean-Marc made the doe bleat calls.

A deer bounded up with a rush from a screening of alders no more than 30 feet in front of us. In a flash I saw the white tail, the big, glistening antlers, the arcing body; and my rifle leaped to my shoulder. I thumbed the safety off just as the crosshairs found the buck's chest as he sailed over a log.

"He heard our calls and came here and waited," Jean-Marc declared when we knelt beside the big 7-point buck. "That's what they do."

I can't be sure, of course, but I came away convinced that a doe bleat call is a helpful tool to use when bucks are in the rut. Using the call sparingly will not scare deer away, and the call may help put you and a trophy buck in the same place at the same time.

14

GETTING
THE
SHOT

"There he is!" Mark whispers. "See him?" The camera pans through the forest, then zooms in on a speck of movement in the distance. The first thing you see is the antlers. They're enormous.

You are right there, looking over Mark's shoulder. You can hear Mark's grunt call and watch the big buck picking his way through the woods, coming closer. Mark draws his bow, and you hear the release and see the arrow zing through the air and bury itself behind the huge buck's shoulder.

This graphic video sequence is only one of more than 120 successful trophy deer hunts brothers Mark and Terry Drury and their team of expert hunters have produced in the past eight years for their three Drury Outdoors hunting film series, *Monster Bucks,* *Whitetail Madness,* and *Dream Seasons.*

It takes a lot more than luck just to pull off that many successful trophy deer hunts, and these hunters must not only make the shot, but also hide a cameraman and get the action on film. Furthermore, they absolutely guarantee that their films show only totally wild deer and that they use 100 percent fair chase hunting methods. No gimmicks. No game farms or private refuges.

The Drury Outdoors hunting team members hunt the same wild whitetail deer the rest of us do. Their advantage over the rest of us is that they know more about how and where to set up for big deer.

"We haven't any secrets," Terry Drury told me. "Come with us. We'll show you what we do."

I joined the Drurys in the deer woods, and this is what I learned:

SCOUTING

These guys start scouting for next year's bucks soon after this year's deer season closes. They want to know right away where big bucks survived and start making plans for hunting those individual deer next year. They continue adding to the information they have gathered by scouting and observing deer movements throughout the summer and fall. Here's how they collect and evaluate information:

- Scout early. Scouting in January and February tells you where mature bucks that survived hunting season are living. Its important to find where the big ones live months before you plan to hunt them.
- Stick to the facts. If deer sign is lacking, deer are not using that location, regardless of how good it looks to you.
- Tracks don't lie. Tracks tell where mature bucks go. Tracks tell you, "He's here." Tracks tell you the size of the deer.

- Big bucks sometimes rub smaller trees, but *only* big bucks rub big trees. During early scouting trips, look for last year's rubs on large trees. In September, check these old rubs for new use, a sure sign that last year's mature buck is still alive and using this territory. Keep notes to remind yourself where large rubs are located.
- Tine marks on secondary trees and shrubs surrounding a rub on a large tree indicate extra wide and long-tined antlers.
- Big bucks make the earliest rubs each autumn. Bucks rub trees to mark territories and strengthen their neck muscles for fighting, and the big boys need to be in fighting condition first.
- Where big bucks have been observed moving in daylight, they will move in daylight again.
- Deer sign is diluted while crops are standing because there is food and cover everywhere and deer are not concentrated. Once crops are cut, deer sign will be concentrated in travel corridors and wooded cover.
- Use U.S. Department of Agriculture and County Farm Bureau aerial photos and plat maps to locate farms that offer a mix of crops and wooded cover. These photos and maps give excellent indications of where deer are likely to bed, travel, and feed. With this advance knowledge, you can save time by scouting the likeliest areas rather than having to walk entire farms.
- Whenever lots of hunters are using rattling antlers and grunt calls, mature bucks become wary of these sounds. That's the time to sit quietly downwind of a buck's bedding area in thick, heavy cover.
- Rain washes the slate clean. Come back after a rain to check for fresh tracks and droppings that show where deer have moved most recently.

HANGING STANDS

Perfect shots occur when a deer and a hunter happen to be in the same place at the same time but the deer doesn't know the hunter is there. The Drury team hunters spend countless hours studying deer movement patterns before zeroing in on where to hang a treestand. Then they take every precaution to keep the deer from knowing where the stand is and when it's being used. Here is the process they follow:

- When first hunting a new area, hang observation stands in places where you can see for long distances. Watch deer movements from these stands for a month or two to learn travel, feeding, and bedding patterns before you decide where to hang stands for hunting.
- Keep written records on every stand you hang. Record the type of habitat it overlooks; the wind directions that favor it; and whether it overlooks a travel corridor, bedding area, feeding area, a buck's home core area, or other special feature. Use this information to decide which stand to hunt from, according to each day's wind direction, and what you expect deer to be doing that day.
- The most frequent mistake made by hunters is that they allow deer to pattern them. Hunters make this mistake when they use the same stand over and over again, and approach and leave the stand at regular times. Deer quickly learn to avoid the stand area when the hunter will be using it. Instead, hunters should hang lots of stands and use them alternately, when the wind favors their locations.
- Hang stands early in July and August. It takes more than a month for mature bucks to get used to changes in their territory and overcome their natural caution about new objects.

- In farm country, hang stands in the woods before corn is cut in the fields. Deer will be living in the high corn and will be less aware of changes made in the wooded cover. Once corn is cut, it's too late to make disturbances in the woods.
- Nobody owns too many stands. You need to hang a different stand for each wind direction, and reserve at least two "floaters" to use when new prospective sites look good.
- Mature bucks don't need much of an excuse to vacate areas where they have been disturbed or have encountered human scent too often.
- Deer are masters at checking scent before they enter an area. Always remember, downwind deer know you are there.
- When hanging stands, wear rubber gloves and rubber boots. Leave as little human scent as possible. When hunting, wear cover scent or wash your clothes in a scent inhibitor.
- It's best to hang stands and cut shooting lanes on a rainy day. Your scent will be washed away sooner.
- Hang stands 18 to 24 feet above the ground and make sure they are not silhouetted against open sky.
- Don't hang stands directly over a concentration of rubs or scrapes that indicate a buck's heavily used home ground. Instead, pull back and hang your stand where it overlooks these sites from downwind roughly 100 yards away. Plan to use rattling antlers or a grunt call to bring a buck into shooting range. Expect to encounter the buck when he circles downwind of his bedding area to scent-check it prior to entering.
- It may require observations over three or four years to figure out precisely the best place to hang a stand in a certain piece of woods. Learn by your mistakes. There is no substitution for observed deer movement.
- Hang stands where your scent will be carried back over an area where you don't expect deer to travel.

- Hang stands high on ridges, not in bottoms. Winds are more consistent on high ground, and mature bucks scent-check hollows by traveling the higher ground above them.
- Use a rangefinder or pace off distances, and mark reference points at 20, 30, and 35 yards so you will know the exact range when a deer comes in.
- Pay attention to where old wooden stands were built. Someone who no longer hunts your area may have already discovered an excellent location for you to hang a stand.
- Little mistakes will cost you big bucks. Clear clean shooting lanes. One little twig is all it takes to deflect a good shot.
- Clear shooting lanes in late winter or early spring, before new growth begins. This will make your lanes look natural by the time hunting season begins.
- Always try to approach your stands from downwind. Go directly in and out, leaving as little scent as possible. Minimize how many deer trails you cross on the way to your stand.
- Be aware of where your scent is being carried at all times.
- Never smoke, spit, or urinate near your stands. Carry a bottle to urinate in while in your stand.
- Rainy days give you a free pass; your scent will be washed away quickly. Rainy days are good times to use a stand close to a buck's bedding area.

DEER BEHAVIOR

Successful hunters never stop learning about deer behavior. Everything a deer does is of interest to them. They demand to know why any deer is where it is at any particular time and use their accumulated knowledge to predict where the deer will go next. Here are some observations the Drury team members say helps them predict where deer will be when:

- Deer are strongly affected by the moon. The majority of does begin their estrus cycle about a week after the Hunter's Moon with the peak of breeding occuring two weeks after the Hunter's Moon. (The Hunter's Moon is the second full moon following the autumn equinox, which occurs about September 21.)

- Be aware of moon phases, and be in your stand whenever the moon is visible during daylight hours. Deer are more active in the daytime when the moon is visible.

- Older bucks are more concerned with survival than with re-production. Expect the biggest bucks to remain bedded in daylight hours until the peak of the rut, when they some-times make mistakes and may be seeking does during shoot-ing hours.

- Bucks settle dominance disputes before the breeding season begins. Rattling antlers and grunt calls are very effective dur-ing this pre-rut period.

- Big bucks rarely use heavily traveled deer trails. Instead, they cut across these trails or check them from the downwind side, seeking the scent of a doe in estrus. Use rattling horns and a grunt-snort-wheeze call to attract a buck to your stand.

- Scrapes are made by bucks of all sizes. The size of the track in the scrape, not the size of the scrape itself, indicates the size of the buck that made it. Bucks approach scrapes from downwind.

- Travel corridors, where several heavily used doe trails join or parallel one another, are patrolled by bucks during the peak of the rut. These are locations where you may see a mature buck trailing a doe during daylight hours.

- Numerous big tree rubs close together mark a mature buck's bedding area. If you find lots of large droppings, large tracks, scrapes, and the impressions of large single beds nearby, you have found the core area where a big buck spends lots of daylight hours. It will be close to thick escape cover, on higher ground, with a good view of the surroundings.

- Deer live on corn in farm country. Mature bucks often remain inside fields of standing corn until it is cut. Where corn is still high during the rut, expect to see bucks along field edges close to cover. Once the corn is cut, mature bucks continue to skirt the field edges searching for hot does, but often travel inside the woods line. Excellent stand locations can be found inside the wooded edge at field corners.

- Pay attention to crop rotations. Deer follow corn plantings and move to new locations according to where corn is planted each year. If rubs along a field edge were made when the field was in corn, bucks will use that edge again next time corn is planted there.

SHOOTING TROPHY DEER

One reason the Drury team hunters continue to rack up big scores on trophy bucks is that they pay careful attention to the habits of younger bucks. When a younger buck matures into a trophy animal, these hunters already know a great deal about where that particular buck spends his time and have fine-tuned their ability to predict his movements. Here are their rules for shooting trophy bucks:

- You can only shoot trophies consistently if you pass up smaller bucks. When a buck comes in that is smaller than what you really want, remember where he travels and plan to hunt him again when he matures. Two-year-old bucks will usually continue to live in the same area when they mature to trophy size. Learning the habits of two-year-old bucks is an important investment for the future.

- Allow smaller deer to pass without letting them detect you. A mature buck may be following.
- Places where bucks enter and leave cornfields are often marked by tree rubs.
- A grunt-snort-wheeze combination call challenges a buck's ego and is the best call to use to pull a mature buck away from a doe.
- Be in your stand before daylight and stay until dark.

15

TROPHY DEER MANAGEMENT

Most deer hunters dream of killing a wall hanger, but should state wildlife agencies make new rules that would prohibit hunters from killing bucks with less than "trophy-size" antlers?

That question is being raised in state deer regulation hearings nationwide, and the concept is being pushed hard by some organized sportsmen's groups.

Those who favor the idea say that if it became illegal to shoot bucks with small antlers, more bucks would grow up to develop large antlers, and hunters would have better chances of seeing trophy deer.

Opponents of the idea say that isn't necessarily true.

In the first place, not every small-antlered buck grows up to have large antlers; some never develop trophy racks due to genetic or nutritional shortcomings. Furthermore, there is no guarantee that a deer that is not shot this year will still be around next year. Many die of disease or starvation; some are killed in highway accidents; others are killed by predators and poachers; and still more deer can be expected to simply move out of the trophy deer management area.

There are also distinct philosophical reasons why many hunters oppose a ban on killing yearling bucks, even if it can produce a greater percentage of big bucks in certain situations.

Some see it as "just one more government regulation."

"Why should I have to pass up a nice young buck that satisfies me so that some 'trophy hunter' has an increased chance to kill something he can brag about?" others question.

"I don't have much time to hunt—if I had to wait for a trophy buck I probably wouldn't get one at all," another declares.

"If it's illegal to shoot a buck with less than a 15-inch antler spread, how can I tell if a rack is 15 inches wide? What if I kill one that is 14 inches or 12 inches by mistake—am I going to lose my hunting license or have the deer or my gun confiscated?" some hunters worry.

"What about my young son," some fathers lament. "Trophy-only regulations lower the chance of his success."

"People think saving young bucks will make it easier to bag bucks with big antlers, but it doesn't work that way. Older deer are smarter deer, and the hunter success rate will actually drop if only older bucks can be harvested," others predict.

As whitetail populations continue to reach new heights in many states, the need to regulate deer harvests in ways that maintain balanced age and sex structures challenges state wildlife agencies. Harvesting antlerless deer allows states to balance the size and sex ratio of their deer herds. When hunting pressure on bucks is high, on the other hand, the age structure of the antlered portion of a deer herd may be badly skewed.

In parts of heavily hunted states such as New Jersey, Maryland, Pennsylvania, Virginia, Vermont, and New York, yearling bucks sometimes make up 80 to 90 percent of the antlered harvest. When so few bucks survive their first year with antlers, how many can be expected to reach their prime?

Since nearly all 1–1/2-year-old bucks have antler spreads of less than 15 inches, banning the killing of smaller-antlered bucks is one way to assure that more bucks will reach at least 2–1/2 years of age before being harvested.

Private deer hunting lodges and clubs that control large tracts of land are in the position to impose voluntary harvest restraints, and can adjust the amount of hunting pressure by limiting their number of clients and members. Many that have done so can show indisputable records proving that prohibiting the killing of yearling bucks, combined with harvesting a quota of does in order to balance the deer population with the habitat, has resulted in more big bucks being taken by their constituents while improving the overall structure of their herd.

Their bible has been a 1975 book called *Producing Quality Whitetails*, by Al Brothers, a former Texas Parks and Wildlife Department biologist who became manager of a large ranch complex, and Murphy E. Ray, Jr. This book outlines the concepts that have become known as Quality Deer Management, or QDM, and demonstrates how hunters can be transformed from consumers into managers by re-evaluating their deer hunting priorities.

The idea has spawned an organization called the Quality Deer Management Association, whose members view yearling bucks as subjects to study and learn from while restricting themselves to shooting only does and older bucks.

The movement has generated a zealous following that is convinced that shooting yearling bucks is unwise. Although the QDMA officially sticks to an education-only role, many of its members are active in trying to move state wildlife agencies toward banning the killing of yearling bucks.

Their battle plan is outlined in a new book, *Quality Whitetails, The Why and How of Quality Deer Management*, by University of Georgia wildlife professors Karl V. Miller and R. Larry Marchinton

(Stackpole, $29.95). The book is "aimed at moving quality deer management out of the realm of the large landowner and into that of the average hunter."

Georgia was the first state to pass regulations that prohibit killing yearling bucks on both public and private land. With "overwhelming support" from surveyed constituents, Georgia outlawed killing bucks with less than 15-inch antler spreads in two counties where experimental deer management policies were in effect and initiated similar restricted buck harvest regulations on 10 percent of public wildlife management units. Comparable changes have been proposed by hunter groups in many other states.

The Georgia experiment is being watched by other state wildlife biologists, some of whom predict that saving yearling bucks will only yield an immediate higher percentage of 2–1/2-year-old bucks in future harvests, but will not result in significant increases of prime 4- and 5-year-old bucks bucks being harvested.

The QDMA folks are quick to respond that increasing the percentage of older bucks is only one of their goals. They also stress that aggressive doe harvests are often needed to keep deer herds in balance with their habitat and are educating people to shoot does rather than young bucks for meat wherever antlerless seasons make that possible.

By educating hunters to think in terms of shaping local deer populations, the QDMA hopes to make hunters see themselves as ethical wildlife managers who cull the part of the herd that needs to be harvested and protect the part they want to have grow.

Is the QDM concept "an idea whose time has come," as its advocates insist?

QDM has proven effective on certain large blocks of private lands where habitat conditions, deer populations, *and hunting pressure* can be controlled by voluntary agreement. Is the deer hunting public ready to accept state regulations that would reduce hunting pressure on bucks at a time when deer populations are reaching record highs?

That is the question whose time is coming.

16

MY MOST MEMORABLE BUCK

As I remember him, he was the biggest buck ever. His antlers soared and glistened, and his neck swelled from his shoulders as big around as an oak sawlog. He had a rump like an ox, legs as sturdy as a young bull, and I can still feel the sweat trickling down my back as I dragged him home through the snow. The smile I wore that day made my face ache. That was fifty years ago.

He was my first and most memorable buck. I can see him clearly to this day rising up from behind that log, so close that *he* scared *me*, and I jumped back from him as he took my measure, then started moving off through the snowy woods. I fought paralysis, forcing the gun up to my shoulder with the same awful helplessness that terrorizes you in a dream when there's a lion on your tail and you can't get your feet moving.

He was enormous, the biggest buck I'd ever seen.

But wait a minute. Writing this has made me curious, and a few minutes ago I went out to dig around in the antler pile that I have accumulated out in the barn. I found the old rack deep down in the heap, hair all worn off the skull plate, and I'm damned if the rack hasn't shrunk.

It's the right rack, I'm sure of that; the year 1950 is written on the skull. But the rack has gotten smaller over the years. I remember it as having 10 points when I shot it. In fact, I kind of thought it had 12. It's only an 8-pointer now. Its massive main beams, once as thick as my wrist, have shrunk down to something about the thickness of my thumb, and the tines aren't half as long as I remember. I should have thrown that old rack away long ago, for the memory of those antlers sure beats the hell out of the shrunken evidence that's out in the horn pile now.

It's worse than that old brook trout I caught with Rob Kilgore up on the Dead Diamond River the year I flunked out of college. Now that was a trout! Four pounds if he was an ounce, long as your arm, and splattered all over with blood-red spots.

I couldn't afford to have him mounted (he was too big), so I kept him for years in Dad's freezer. Every once in a while when talking about him, I'd go over and dig the old fish out to show people. As the years passed, he shrank, too, and lost his color. His sides caved in, his tail curled and finally broke off, and in the end he wasn't half as good to look at as his story was to tell. The best thing I ever did was feed him to the cat, and that's what I ought to do with those damned horns, too.

I'll tell you about this buck just the way he lives in recollection, and to hell with the horns.

I'd seen him several times that summer coming out to feed along the edge of an alfalfa field just at the last squeak of daylight. He'd appear at the upper corner of the field and stand there for a long time looking things over before he'd mosey out. I saw him twice that autumn, too, when my Gordon setter Lady and I headed up the hill after school to look for grouse along the top of the ravine.

December came and with it the opening of deer season. The law required buckshot only and a gun of at least 12 gauge, so my sweet 16-gauge bird gun was of no use now. I took the last $15 of my trapping money and invested it in the only deer gun I could afford, a rusty 12-gauge Stevens double that bordered on being antique. It had a loose forend and doubled—that is, both barrels went off simultaneously whenever one was triggered.

I steel-wooled the rust off and reblued the barrels with a bottled solution that didn't change the color of the barrels much, but made the gun smell loudly of rotten eggs.

The first few days of deer season were dry and cold, and the woods were brittle and noisy. Then it started to snow. The storm blew all Thursday night and all day Friday, dumping a foot, a foot and a half, finally two feet of snow over the countryside. On Saturday morning I was up early, dressed for the arctic. By dawn's first light I was in the woods, heading for the big ravine where the cedars grew thick and honeysuckle vines festooned the trees, giving shelter from the storm.

Moving silently through the deep snow, creeping into the wind, I came up on the deer undetected. They were bedded in the thick stuff, only their heads showing above the snow, but the big buck was not with them.

I moved on down through the cedars into a hollow along the creek and had not gone far when I spotted him. He was standing in a honeysuckle thicket with his rump to the wind. Though I couldn't clearly see his antlers, I knew this was the big buck by the mighty breadth of his haunches and the solid look of him.

I knelt in the snow, then started forward on my knees so that the snow pushed up against my stomach and only the top half of me was showing. Silently I closed with the big buck. He was out of my view now, but I knew just where he was standing about 100 yards ahead, and I crept toward him with my pulse pounding in my ears and my eyes streaming tears from staring into the wind.

Shivering with tension, I crept into the thicket with him, knowing that when I next saw him he would be close enough to shoot. I moved with my thumb on the safety, the old gun held across my chest, ready to spring to my shoulder. I crept on and on, until it seemed I must be right on top of him, yet I saw nothing—no deer, no tracks. He had vanished without a trace. I knew I was kneeling within a few feet of where the buck had been, yet there was no sign of him.

Confused, I stood up.

With that, the buck jumped to its feet, rising in a rush from the other side of a thick log no more than a dozen feet away. He scared me, jumping up like that so close, and then turning to stare at me before beginning to move away. I forced the gun up, overcoming waves of paralyzing buck fever. As he turned broadside, I got the bead on his chest and touched off the old gun.

True to form, the gun doubled, and when the paired loads of high-brass buckshot went off, the gun kicked back, bloodying my nose. The fore-end flew off into the snow and the breech flew open. But that didn't matter now, for the big buck was down. I plucked the empty hulls out of the gun and groped in my pocket for a pair of fresh loads. My eye was on the deer, which now was struggling to rise. Quickly, I shoved in the new hulls with my gloved hand and slammed the breech closed. But as I did so, the heel of my glove caught and was pinched in the breech when it locked shut. Caught in that position, my hand stuck on the top of the barrel, I couldn't reach the triggers with my fingers. Nor could I get a thumb back to the tang to open the jammed gun and free my gloved hand. All the time the big buck was drifting off, his antlers getting bigger with each step he took away from me. And my gun was jammed. I couldn't shoot!

I ran to the nearest tree and smacked the old gun against the trunk, trying to hammer it open. Finally, after several smacks, I succeeded and the gun fell apart in my hands. The barrels separated from the breech and fell in the snow, because the fore-end was already gone and there was nothing to hold the gun together.

I fitted the barrels back into the breech, got the shells in place once more, and gently closed the gun and heard it click into locked position. Then, my eye still on the escaping buck, I thrashed through the snow behind him and finally, because he was mortally hit and and losing strength fast, I caught up with him and blew the old gun apart a second time, administering the coup.

My God, he was a mighty buck that day! The shriveled old antlers I have out in the barn bear no resemblance to the thick beams that filled my hands as I dragged him through the snow toward home. Antlers that went on forever. I couldn't stop admiring them. And shoulders! Why, they just don't make deer like that anymore!

I ate him all that winter. Mom and Dad thought he was tough, but he didn't seem tough to me. I remember his meat was tender as filet mignon and tastier than any critter raised on corn. Deer meat and beans! Now there was food for a man to grow on. Food to make a man dream and start making plans about the way things were going to be in life. Food to make a man capable of getting his priorities in line.

Just you never mind about those puny horns out in my antler heap; that deer was huge the day I shot him, and he's been getting bigger ever since.

17

FIRST
DEER

We had just finished helping old Fred Pickett hang a nice 8-pointer on the meatpole up at deer camp when Fred reached in his pocket, then held out his hand and showed us an odd-looking little piece of meat.

"See that?" he asked. "That's the tongue off my deer. First thing I do when I shoot a deer is cut its tongue off and put it in my pocket. I been doin' that ever since I was 14 years old."

Then he told us this story.

"I killed my first deer when I was 14," he said, "but it was stolen by some older guys who came and took it away from me.

"I was up on a little mountain where I had my trapline about a mile from home. I'd seen a line of buck and rubs up there, and before the season opened I made a rough blind out of branches around a stump, which I sat on.

"I was in my blind and sitting on my stump before daylight on Opening Day. I had an old 12-gauge shotgun with 0-Buck in the right barrel, 00-Buck in the left, and six more buckshot loads in my pocket. I had already picked out trees I knew were 30 yards from where I sat and marked them in my mind. If a buck came past one of those marks, I would know he was in killing range.

"About 8 o'clock that morning a buck did come along, and when he passed one of my marks I dropped him. He was a 6-pointer, and I was proud enough to bust. I just sat there in the leaves touching him and looking at him. It had been a good, clean kill, and I was proud of that. That was the way I swore I'd always do it, let 'em come real close and then drop 'em dead.

"I had dragged the buck over to a little rise of ground and had him on his back, and was just beginning to cut him open when I heard somebody coming through the woods. Turned out to be two men I'd never seen before. They were great big guys with automatic shotguns and red wool suits with their pants tucked into their boots. One of 'em was smoking a cigar.

"They came right up to where I was and the one with the cigar says, 'I see you shot one of our deer.'

"I shot *this* deer," I said.

"Well, he's our deer," says Cigar. "You shot him off our drive. We've got a big drive goin' on this mountain right now. We pushed him to you."

"He just came through the woods to me," I said. "I didn't hear any drive. Anyway, what difference does it make if you had a drive going?"

"It makes all the difference," Cigar says, blowing smoke. "Any deer that gets killed off our drive is our deer."

"Now, you just hold that hind leg while I finish dressin' this deer," the other one told me.

"So I held the leg and they finished dressing the deer and then Cigar tells the other guy, 'Put your tag on it. Let's get this thing outta here.'

"I was just a little kid and they were big. There wasn't a thing I could do," Fred recalled. "I just stood there and watched them drag my deer away.

"I called the game warden as soon as I got home, but it was nighttime before he called me back. I told him what happened. He said 'Son, that's too bad, but there's nothing I can do about it because we can't identify your deer. There's no way I can tell your deer from any other that gets checked in.'

"Then the warden told me this: whenever you kill a deer, cut its tongue off and put it in your pocket. Then, if somebody steals the deer from you, you've always got a way to identify it.

"I've been cuttin' the tongues off deer and carryin' them around in my pocket ever since. After all these years I still never feel a deer is really mine until he's back at camp, hanging on my meatpole, with my tag on him and his tongue is in my pocket."

18

CANOEING FOR MULE DEER

Rocky Mountain deer hunting is expected to be a horseback or 4-wheel-drive proposition. Drop into any little cowboy bar during hunting season and you'll learn that in a hurry.

My gang stopped one October night in a little joint in Wyoming with a view of the Big Horn range on one side and the Absarokas on the other and ordered beers. The cowboys spotted us as Easterners right away.

"Goin' huntin'?" one asked, winking broadly at his buddy.

"Better have rigs with winches on the front," the other chimed in. "You're in rough country and the bucks are way up under the rimrock."

Then they looked out the window and saw the canoes on top of our trucks.

"Canoes," they both guffawed, slapping their knees and wagging their Stetsons in mock despair. "Hell, boys, you can't go huntin' in them!"

That was the general reaction wherever we went. Everybody out there thought of canoes as tippy little play toys that people fool around in when it's hot. The idea that grown men would actually paddle canoes down a Wyoming river in pursuit of deer struck them as a typical example of damn fool Eastern thinking.

"Best take your water wings," we were cautioned.

"Ain't no real deer on the river, anyway," one of the cowboys declared. "The bucks are still way up where only a man on a horse or a man with a good four-wheelin' rig can get at 'em."

We were a laughingstock, but we didn't mind, because we had already paddled one short stretch of the river and had seen lots of deer sign on the islands and in the brushy cover that choked the insides of the sweeping river bends. We knew that the local boys with their eyes set on the mountain peaks and their rear ends deep in their saddles and bucket seats were overlooking some very heavy concentrations of deer.

"There's nothin' but does and little fawn deer along the river," we were advised. But if that was true, some of those does had awfully big feet and nurtured a curious habit of rubbing the bark off big saplings and making scrapes where head-high branches overhung the network of riverbank trails.

We listened to the cowboys solemnly, sipped our beers, and said little. The season would open in the morning.

We breakfasted at a truck stop out on the highway before daylight. The four-wheel drive boys were roaring past headed for the high country, and pickups pulling horse trailers whizzed by, piloted by men with fluorescent-orange covers on their cowboy hats. I doubt there was another canoe atop a vehicle that day in the whole state of Wyoming.

We slid our canoes down a steep embankment just at dawn. The current was steady, the river slow and deep. There were no rapids or rocks and few overhanging trees. Even a cowboy could have paddled down this stretch.

The floodplain on both shores was grown up in brush and cottonwood groves. Sometimes the brushy strip was only a few yards wide, but at bends it would widen out so that the strip became perhaps a quarter mile wide on one bank or the other. Here and there above the floodplain were big fields of alfalfa, corn, and grain stubble.

About a mile downstream we came to a long timbered point with a sign on it proclaiming that this was public land. There was evidence that fishermen came here in summer, but their boot marks had long since disappeared. The only tracks were those of deer and raccoons.

"Hard to believe there's any deer left up in the high country," Jim Henry whispered. "It looks to me like they're all right here."

"These deer have probably never been hunted," Harry Baxter said. "Nobody hunts by boat out here."

The amount of deer sign was unbelievable. We knew enough to recognize that wherever does were concentrated next to feed and cover during the rut, bucks had to be there, too. The large tracks and rubs on big saplings assured us that they weren't all just little guys, either.

Harry had lived in Wyoming for the past 11 years, but he is a transplant to the Cowboy State from Maine and New Hampshire where he grew up in the canoe tradition. Harry had always used canoes for hunting, so when he moved West he naturally put his canoeing skills to work and found that he had the state's whole wilderness waterway system to himself in hunting season. Each year Harry uses his canoe to reach remote country that is overlooked or accessible only by water. He bags his deer, elk, and antelope every year.

Harry's son-in-law, Bill Terry, is a Wyoming native, all cowboy hat, horse trailer, and four on the floor, but under his young wife's and Harry's influence, Bill has seen the light and become a canoeist, too. Bill still hunts the high country with a horse when he's with his own crowd, but this time he had joined up with us, big hat, high-heeled boots and all.

The rest of our bunch were canoe hunting friends from back East who didn't know enough to overlook the Wyoming low country.

We put two men off at a shallow riffle crossing where a deer trail three feet wide came out of the timber. Our two snipers crawled into natural hides amidst the flood-piled logs and brush on the riverbank. The rest of us paddled half a mile or so downstream, then beached the canoes and began stillhunting through the timber strip back toward our stationary shooters. It was thick cover and we could rarely see very far ahead, but every now and then we would hear brisk movement in the brush ahead, or see the flash of a mule deer's rump as it went rabbit-hopping away in front of us. Eventually, first one and then the other gun spoke up at the crossing.

We hadn't been on the river for an hour and already two mule deer bucks lay dead on the bank. One was a big 4 × 5 and the other was a wide-racked 3-point. Not record-book bucks, to be sure, but darned good ones. I've met a lot of high-country hunters who have been satisfied with smaller ones. The bucks were butter fat, tenderly fitted out on alfalfa and corn.

"These deer will make those high-country sagebrush eaters taste rank," Harry chuckled. "You couldn't grow better meat than this in a Kansas feed lot."

I won't go into how and when each man shot his buck. Suffice it to say that in two trips down the same 15-mile stretch of river, on two successive mornings, five of our party of seven killed their bucks, and on the third morning the remaining two hunters scored with two more. We hunted only on islands that our maps designated as publicly owned, not private land. Our biggest buck was a wideracked Western count 6-pointer, yet all of the bucks we shot carried three points or more by Western count, and had racks more than two feet wide. Each was in superb condition.

Hunting the islands and river crossings, we saw numerous other antlered deer each day, but we passed up spikes and forkhorns, waiting for deer with heavier racks to show.

In our three days on the river, we actually spent more time paddling dead deer out to the pickups than we spent hunting. It was very pleasant sliding down the quiet river with the snowy peaks in the background and a couple of big bucks piled amidships. Although it was mid-October and we had occasional light snow, the weather was fine for canoeing. There was no ice, no rapids, and deer sign was everywhere.

"We were lucky," Bill Terry admitted. "It isn't always that easy."

Nevertheless, the low riverbank country holds a large deer population. In the daytime the deer are concentrated in the brushy strips along shore and on the numerous brush-covered islands. When a couple of hunters stillhunt slowly through the thick, brushy cover, the deer move ahead and break into the open at easily identified river crossings where a waiting rifleman has a clear shot.

"The does, fawns, and smaller bucks usually break out and cross first," Bill explained. "We got the bigger bucks because we let the smaller ones pass and waited. When the bigger bucks finally broke out we were ready."

Hunting the rivers of Wyoming is so unusual that we drew a small crowd of local spectators each time we paddled into the little town and began unloading deer from the canoes.

"Damnedest thing I ever seen," one Marlboro Man type said, blowing smoke. "I never knew there were bucks like that right down here along the river."

Several times we saw bucks that had larger antlers than any we shot. I remember one old campaigner that we glassed as he lay in his bed in high grass along the riverbank, just below the edge of a big alfalfa field. His antlers stuck up like mesquite brush and glistened in the sun when he turned his head. Unfortunately, he was on private property where we did not have permission to hunt, so we had to pass him up. Another time we watched a herd of antlerless deer feeding on alfalfa close to the river. As we watched, four bucks with almost-identical wide and heavy 4-point racks shouldered up from a river crossing and stood just inside the edge of the timber, watching the does. These were also on private property, so we could not go after them, but seeing them added to our knowledge that there are plenty of good bucks—deer that would make most hunters proud— at canoe elevation.

Over the years Harry Baxter and a few of his friends have hunted widely on Wyoming's rivers. Harry gets an elk every year by paddling before daylight deep into a zone where horseback hunters and hunters coming in off roads unknowingly drive elk ahead of them. The elk eventually cross a narrow belt of timber where Harry waits not far from his canoe. Field-dressing the elk on the spot, Harry packs the meat out by canoe and is usually home before the horseback hunters get out of the woods.

He gets his antelope every year by canoeing small tributary rivers across the plains until he is far from a road. Then he beaches his canoe, peeks over the riverbank, and looks for an antelope herd.

"They often bed during the day near a remote river," he explains. "Antelope expect trouble to come from roads and get up and run whenever they see a vehicle coming. But they are not usually hunted from the rivers, so they feel safe near remote watercourses. I just paddle as close as I can to a bedded herd. I often get close enough to shoot from the riverbank.

A vast portion of Wyoming is publicly owned land administered by either the U.S. Forest Service, Bureau of Land Management (BLM), or U.S. Park Service. National forests and BLM lands are generally open to hunting and even parts of the national parks can be hunted during special seasons. All of the major rivers in Wyoming—the Big Horn, Shoshone, Snake, Green, North Platte, Wind, and many tributaries—pass through large tracts of public land where hunting is permitted and abundant herds of deer, elk, and antelope reside.

To avoid putting too much pressure on any single area, I have not named the river on which we had our success. But that is not the only reason for being non-specific. The truth is that canoe hunting can be so successful on any of Wyoming's canoeable waterways that there is no reason to draw attention to one river and make it sound better than the others.

When we applied for nonresident Wyoming hunting licenses, we requested zones through which canoeable waterways crossed ample public land. We made those choices according to what anyone can see by looking at a map. Before hunting, we traveled to those zones to scout the area before deciding which stretch of river we would run.

19

GUIDED BY LEWIS AND CLARK

Nothing boosts a deer hunter's confidence like the sight of lots of deer tracks in a big chunk of empty country. The riverbank near the place where we set up camp was so profusely cut by overlapping deer tracks that we stumbled on the pitted earth as we carried our gear from the canoes up to our tent site. The willows in back of the tents were brightly scarred with buck rubs.

"We're right on some old buck's stomping grounds," Chris declared. He was right. Late that night we were awakened by a deer snorting very close to the tents, and in the morning another fresh rub had appeared on a thick willow not 40 feet away.

We were probing the stark, deserted country known as the Missouri Breaks in north-central Montana. Four of us had traveled upstream by canoe on the 149-mile section of the Missouri River between Fort Peck Reservoir and Fort Benton, an area which has been preserved and made public by the National Scenic River Act. Our maps from the Bureau of Land Management showed hundreds of square miles of public land paralleling both sides of the river.

We had selected this stretch of the river for our hunt because it was right here where Lewis and Clark reported seeing more game than they had ever encountered on their exploration of the territory in 1805. In fact, the campsite we had chosen was the same site from which the Lewis and Clark party had conducted a hunt that provided an impressive quantity of venison.

"Doesn't look like anybody's been here since Lewis and Clark left," Jim said. "There's no sign of other people camping here, and I've never seen so many deer tracks in one place."

A sage- and grass-covered floodplain extended for half a mile on either side of the river, ending at the foot of crenelated walls of steep sandstone and glacial clay that rose straight up for almost 1,000 feet. The walls were spilt in all directions by sharply eroded canyons crowned by wind-sculpted minarets and sparsely dressed with stands of twisted pine and juniper. Along the riverbanks were willow brakes, groves of ancient cottonwoods, and impenetrable thickets of prickly wild rose. Wherever private ranchland penetrated the vast public land holdings, patches of bright green alfalfa provided an extra rich alternative food supply for the burgeoning deer population.

"There's whitetail deer and pheasants close to the river and mule deer and sharptail grouse in the hills," an enthusiastic salesman in the Lewistown sporting goods store had told us as he sold us licenses and extra antlerless deer permits. We walked out of the store with licenses for three deer apiece.

"If we limit out we're going to sink the canoes," Jim worried.

"We'll just make extra trips till we get 'em all out to the trucks," Matt countered.

Matt's eagerness was understandable. He had not been drawn for a big game license, so he had just come along to supply the rest of us with rabbits, pheasants, and sharptails to eat while we hunted deer. We had promised Matt a full share of the venison, so he was keen to have us fill the boats with deer.

An hour before dawn we were awakened by coyotes singing in the hills.

"We've got all the amenities," Matt yawned. "Even a coyote alarm clock."

As the eastern sky brightened, we headed off in different directions to hunt. Matt and his Bozeman buddy Chris crossed the river to hunt on the other side, while Jim slipped into the willows to hunt for whitetails. I elected to climb into the hills and see what I could see. Each of us carried a hand-held CB radio so we could stay in touch and hear what the others were finding.

By midmorning I was up among the sandstone minarets looking over a narrow, sparsely timbered draw in which I had spotted a mule deer doe bedded with two fawns. There were ancient trails everywhere that had been worn to fine dust by heavy deer traffic.

I didn't want to be heard when I turned on my radio, so I dropped back away from the edge of the draw and crawled down into a hole that had been eroded into the sandstone.

"I've got deer running all around me here, but I can't see 'em in the thick willows," I heard Jim whisper. "All I've seen that I could have shot is three ruffed grouse."

Then Matt, who was limited to bird hunting, came on the air.

"I haven't seen a single gamebird," he said. "But I just ran into a huge whitetail buck. He was only 30 yards away and he just stood there looking at me. It was like he knew I couldn't shoot him."

Chris never came on the air, so we figured he was probably sneaking up on one. We agreed to talk again at noon.

I climbed higher until I came out on the top of the Breaks and could see for many miles to the distant, shining Rocky Mountains.

The country around me looked like crumpled brown paper. Jumbled draws and canyons fell off in every direction. There was no flat terrain, only slopes so steep you had to keep one hand on the ground as you climbed. Below me, in the distance, the broad Missouri River flowed in sweeping bends.

In this arid country tracks and droppings last for months, so a profusion of deer tracks can be made by a small bunch of deer traveling the same routes repeatedly. But I was finding fresh droppings everywhere, a sure sign that lots of deer were living here. Each time I peeked over the ridgeline I expected to see a buck, but I was seeing only antlerless deer. I was carrying two antlerless deer permits, but I didn't want to shoot and scare off the bucks I was sure were nearby.

"We'll get our bucks first," we had agreed. "We can fill the antlerless tags after we've got the big fellas hung up in camp."

That evening Chris reported that he had found a mother lode of deer in a big draw. He had seen a lot of deer, including some big bucks, but they were already bedded on the other side of the draw when he got there, so he couldn't approach them.

"Tomorrow I'm going to circle high and come down on the other side of the big draw and be waiting in their bedding area when they show up," he told us. "I'll be needing help dragging a big buck out of there about noon."

Jim wanted me to hunt with him in the thick willows the next day. "You can't see twenty feet in there," he said. "I kept hearing deer hopping around me, but I couldn't see 'em. If two of us moved through there 100 yards apart, we'd be sure to jump deer past each other."

The next morning, just after sunrise, Jim set up a spotting scope and began scanning the hills across the river.

"Whoops," I heard him mutter. "Our plan just went to hell. Look at this guy."

I peered into the 20-power scope and caught my breath. Right in the center stood a mule deer buck with antlers that wouldn't stop. Rather than branching in typical mule deer forks, this rack had points sticking out all over the place. His antlers were at least 30 inches wide! The buck was a mile away, catching the sunrise from a little opening in the trees on a sandstone promontory surrounded by sheer canyon walls.

"We can't pass him up," Jim said. "Let's make a plan."

We all crossed the river and took separate draws, attempting to find routes that would get us above the buck without being seen. But as soon as we got into the draw we all started jumping bands of does and fawns that bounded off with white rumps flashing, warning of danger to all eyes that watched from the hills.

By the time we climbed into rifle range of the big buck's hangout, he was long gone.

"We shoulda shot some of those does," Chris said.

"Woulda scared the buck," Jim countered.

"We scared him anyway," Chris concluded.

Chris killed a wide-antlered 4-point mulie buck on the morning of the third day, just as he had planned. He had climbed to the ridge overlooking the big draw where he had seen the deer the first day and peeked over the top to find three big bucks on parade about 200 yards below him.

"This one looked just about right," he said, stroking his buck's heavy shoulder. He and Matt spent the rest of the day getting the buck out of the hills and back across the river to camp.

One morning Jim, Matt, and I took the big canoe and motored up the river for 20 miles or so, scouting the country. We didn't need more places to hunt—we already had deer all around us—but when you're in new country, you like to get out and see more of it.

That day we spotted a full-curl bighorn ram marching along in bright sunlight on a sidehill above the river. We stopped to explore several abandoned homesteads where settlers had once attempted to wrest their living from this harsh and unforgiving land. Hunting up one barren draw I came upon the weathered frame of a long-abandoned, hand-dug mine shaft where a hopeful old-timer had once burrowed deep into the earth in search of riches that had evaded him above ground.

Now empty of human habitation and seemingly an unspoiled wilderness, it was hard to imagine that this had once been a busy route that thousands of settlers used as a portal to the West. Paddlewheel steamers traveled this stretch of the Missouri all the way to Fort Benton back in the days when the West was being opened.

The river flows smooth and wide, and there are no rapids or rocks to imperil canoes or small boats. Even the places marked "rapids" on our maps turned out to be only shallow spots where steamboats once had to proceed with caution.

On the fourth morning Matt and Chris announced that they missed their lady friends too much to stay any longer. They loaded Chris's buck in one canoe and went home, leaving Jim and me to continue the hunt.

That afternoon we tagged two big does to guarantee some winter meat. We went buck hunting again the next morning.

I went high looking for the big mule deer buck we had scoped across the river, and Jim went back into the willow brush to sit and wait for a whitetail buck. His plan was to watch a small clearing that was crossed by several heavily used deer trails.

That day the wind nearly blew me off the mountain. The Alberta Clipper, as Montana people call it, swooped down out of the north, and the temperature dropped 30 or 40 degrees in an hour. It brought spitting snow and drove yellow sheets of sand against the canyon walls, resuming the sculpting process that had shaped the sandstone minarets.

Miserable as it was, I knew that the deer would be seeking shelter from this wind, and I had a pretty good idea where The Big One would go.

I had discovered the bedding area of a large single deer just under the rim of a short box canyon that I knew would be protected from this wind. I thought I could climb over a ridge, come down into the canyon from the top, and surprise the big buck in his bed.

The wind pelted me with hard snow and sand as I climbed. At times I had to crawl to keep from being blown away.

It was midmorning by the time I was able to reach the rim and peek over the top. When I did, I found myself face to face with two does that saw me at once and leaped from their beds and fled down into the canyon. Then I saw movement in the trees. There was a flash of heavy antlers, then a large body running low.

I caught a glimpse of the buck when it broke from the trees on the far side of the canyon and bounded across a tiny opening, but he flew over the rim of the canyon before I even had time to shoulder my rifle. I will never forget the sight of the wide rack silhouetted briefly against the sky before he disappeared.

Jim killed his buck on our last morning. We had gone high again, sure that the bucks were there. Jim was sneaking through the bottom of a narrow canyon when a buck suddenly jumped from its bed on a slope above him. Just as it started to run, Jim fired.

I heard the shot, and after a few minutes I called Jim on the radio from my perch up among the minarets.

"What'd you shoot?" I asked.

"Two point mulie," he came back.

"Eastern count or Western?" I questioned.

"Both," he said. "He's only got one horn."

That last evening we both took stands overlooking draws that led down to the river, hoping to see deer moving to water before dark. Nothing moved within my sight, but when I got back to camp, Jim was excited.

"Two of the biggest whitetail bucks I've ever seen," Jim reported. (He still had an either-sex tag left.) "They came out of the draw just before dark and moved along the edge of the bare hills. They were half a mile away, so I couldn't shoot, and it was too late to go after them, but I watched them through binoculars. They both had rocking chair racks.

"If we could just stay one more day we could get 'em," he insisted. "We could get out in the sagebrush downwind of where they come out early in the afternoon and just wait for 'em. We could get 'em both."

Unfortunately, we were on a schedule that could not be changed. We had to leave next morning, big bucks or not.

"Damn," Jim said. "We're only just beginning to understand this country and get a feeling for where the deer move, and now it's time to go. You shouldn't come on a trip like this unless you can stay and hunt until you're done—that's the only way to do it."

Outside the tent a coyote yipped in the hills; another chimed in.

"Listen to them laughing," Jim said. "They know that people never stay in this country long enough to find their dreams. People come, scratch around on the surface, and then leave with little or nothing to show for their efforts. It's the way it's always been here."

We loaded up and headed downriver early the next morning. Just before we left, Jim set up his spotting scope one last time and scanned the hills across the river.

"There he is," he said at once. A mile away, high up at the top of the canyon, the big mule deer buck was standing right where we had seen him before. He seemed to be staring down at us.

"Have a nice winter," Jim said, saluting the buck. "Eat well and grow those antlers even bigger. I want to come back and check on you again next fall."

20

TOBACCO ON THE WATER

Bozo St. Onge was reading the signs. "Woman moose," he said, pointing at the line of big heart-shaped tracks in the sand. "Here, boy moose," he said, pointing to some larger slotted tracks.

Then Bozo left the beach and plunged into the fringe of willows at the edge of the floodplain. A line of huge splayed tracks, bigger than dinner plates, marked the trail that paralleled the river. "Big man moose walk here," Bozo said respectfully. "Grandfather moose. Horns like this," he said, spreading his arms above his head.

Jim Henry, Alfred Balch, and I had joined Bozo and his brothers to hunt moose on their ancestral hunting and trapping grounds in the Port Cartier Reserve, north of the Gulf of St. Lawrence in eastern Quebec. The St. Onges are French-speaking Montagnais Indians who guide one party of moose hunters each September.

Lucien St. Onge now took a pouch of Player's Navy Cut tobacco from the pocket of a canvas coat embroidered with animal
pictures.

"Montagnais people believe tobacco strong medicine for
moose hunting," he explained. "Each day spread some tobacco on
the land, spread some on the water. Thank the Great Spirit for the
mountains and the lakes and the rivers and the forest and all the animals and fish. Spread more tobacco and say you know the Great
Spirit has lots of moose. Say if He can spare one moose, please send
it to you. Spread more tobacco. Very good medicine."

Lucien passed the tobacco and each of us spread some on the
land and water and said the words Lucien had instructed. He was
pleased. He smiled at us and said, "Maybe Great Spirit will send you
a moose."

"Hope it's a 60-incher," Alfred said. "We forgot to put that in."

Paul Blacksmith, a very large Montagnais man, was seated on a
log at the edge of the water fashioning a moose call out of a sheet of
white birch bark. He formed it into a funnel with a one-inch hole at
one end and a six-inch opening at the other. Then he bound it with
duct tape and turned it to dry in the smoke of our lunch fire.

"Errunnh," he breathed through the call when it was done.
The sound echoed out across the water. Paul listened to the echo
and nodded. "Good," he said, then helped himself to a bowl of eider
duck soup from the pot on the fire, a slab of bannock, and a mug of
warm tea.

"Is that the best kind of moose call?" I asked.

"Not for me," Homer St. Onge answered. "Paul does it the old
way with a birchbark horn, but I'm a New Age Indian. I call moose
with a chain saw.

"I go on the lake when it's still," he explained. "Pull the chainsaw starting rope. *Purrrrr.* Pull again and the saw starts. Squeeze the

gas. *Rrrrrrhh*. Shut it off. That's it. Moose hear that. From far away it sounds like a woman moose calling for love."

Then Alfred got out his moose call. It was a Maxwell House coffee can with a dampened skate lace dangling through a small hole in the bottom.

He pinched the skate lace between his forefinger and thumbnail and pulled, causing a friction vibration that was amplified by the can. It made a moaning sound, something like a cow moose.

"I call that the Maxwell House Moan," he said. "Good moose call."

The Montagnais people are noted for being especially clean in their habits, and have a reputation for cooking good food. In their neat log cabin on Lac Pasteur that night, the St. Onge brothers served us very delicate, herb-flavored meatballs over pasta.

"What meat is this?" I asked. It was pale in color and delicious.

Bozo reached for the right English words. "Small . . . cow . . . boy," he answered slowly.

Alfred's jaw dropped. "You say we're eatin' cowboy?" he exclaimed.

It took a minute to figure out Bozo's interpretation. "Hold on, Alfred," I said. "He means a small boy cow. In other words, a bull calf. It's veal."

It rained all the next day and the moose stayed in the cover of the forest. If our calls were heard, they were not answered.

"We better tell the Great Spirit a 50-inch bull would be okay," Jim said as we spread tobacco on the water the third morning. "We don't want to seem greedy about that 60-incher."

That day we patrolled the full length of the lake, some 18 miles, and checked for sign. Big granite mountains loomed above us spouting spectacular waterfalls charged by the rain. Moose tracks were everywhere, but most were several days old.

"Moose not moving now," Paul said. "Too warm."

We called anyway, whenever we found a good place that overlooked a big swamp or a long expanse of shoreline. Twice we saw cow moose with calves, but no bulls trailed them. It was so still we could hear ducks splashing from a mile away. Loons yodeled on the lake at night and geese flew overhead honking. Once we heard the lonesome howl of a timber wolf. But no moose spoke.

"We really don't need a big man moose," Alfred said looking skyward as he spread tobacco at dawn on the fourth morning. "If you can spare a nice 35- or 40-incher, that would be fine."

The Montagnais were not dismayed by the lack of moose. They knew it was only a matter of time before the weather would turn colder, triggering the moose breeding season. Then the men moose would be listening for the voices of lovesick women moose and they would come grunting to the call. It was only a matter of time, but our time was running out. We had only two days left.

Though they went unanswered, Paul made lusty and compelling calls through his birchbark horn. He would close his eyes and listen to sounds only he could hear, then raise the birchbark horn to his mouth and pour out swooning cow moose moans so passionate that no man moose worth his antlers could resist them. *Errrunnnh*. He added a lubricious little tremor at the end that sounded perky and flirtatious. He repeated the call three times, adding lilting notes, then ending with the throaty cough of a sexy cow moose with a pond lily stuck in her throat. Finally, he filled the birchbark horn with water, then emptied it into the lake through the small end, simulating the sound of a cow moose urinating. Paul would nod with satisfaction when his performance was finished and turn to us to sense our appreciation, like a Montagnais Pavarotti concluding a much-loved aria.

That night the skies cleared and the wind began pushing brisk waves down the lake. Overhead, northern lights flickered in the sky and hung in ribbons of green and pink that shimmered and whooshed through the heavens. We stood with the St. Onges on the lakeshore and watched the display.

"Love lights in the sky," Bozo called them, turning up his collar against the cold wind. "Tonight the moose will walk."

Back inside the warm cabin the St. Onges spoke quietly to each other in their native tongue. With their hands they gestured, always pointing north.

Then Lucien turned to us and said, "We move in the morning. Take the big tent and move north in the canoes to the end of the lake. Hunt on the river in a big valley where there's lots of moose."

We had completed the journey by noon the next day. The big canvas wall tent was erected in the woods beside a sandy beach at the north end of the lake. The St. Onges cut and laid a deep bed of fir boughs, and we stacked firewood behind the stove.

"Now we go watch," Bozo said. "Later we call."

We canoed up the river a for a mile or so, then climbed a steep granite outcrop that gave us a broad look at the country. From the top we could see the river winding down from the north through a wide valley with open patches where ancient oxbows had grown up in grass. We could see beaches crisscrossed with fresh moose tracks at every river bend. Openings where beavers had cleared away birch and poplar saplings gave more views where moose might be sighted. We took stands close together watching in all directions and waited.

At 3 o'clock Paul called. He called again at 4:00 and 5:00 and 6:00, but no moose stirred. As shooting light faded to darkness we made our way down to the canoes and paddled back to camp.

"Tomorrow," said Homer St. Onge. "Tomorrow is the day."

That night we slept in a row, Indian style, on the bough bed in the big tent. It didn't matter if anyone snored because everyone snored. Nobody slept much. We were up and out before daylight.

"We still holdin' out for a big one?" Jim inquired.

"No," I said. "It's our last day. Any male moose will do now."

As we spread the tobacco that morning and expressed our thoughts, Alfred said, "We don't need a trophy bull. You can't eat horns, anyway."

By late morning we had motored several miles up the river and now were drifting back down with the motor shut off, calling occasionally in hopes of either getting an answer or encountering a bull moose moving on the riverbank. Bozo nodded at us from the stern, keen-eyed, expectant. We drifted in silence, all of us sensing that something was about to happen.

When the bull appeared, he was trotting toward the canoe as if he had been sent to meet us. He wasn't the trophy bull we had imagined when we planned this trip. This was a young bull with small antlers. But he was fat and heavy, just the kind the Montagnais, who shoot for meat, not self-esteem, prize most highly.

Jim, in the bow, raised his rifle and dropped the bull with a single shot.

When we approached the dead moose, Bozo knelt beside it and put his hand on its head. "Thank you for your life," he said seriously.

Then Lucien said, "Perfect moose for eating. Nothing better. When a hunt ends well, we spread tobacco to show we are grateful."

Once again we passed the pouch and spread tobacco on the land and water.

"I respect this ritual," Alfred said. "It makes you realize that honoring the animal you kill is more important than how big its antlers are."

21

MOOSIN' AROUND

"**S**orry about your guide, Marcel," the outfitter apologized to me. "He was so excited about going with you on this trip that he, uh, well, he got drunk. You'll have to stay in my cabin tonight. Tomorrow Marcel will be okay and you can begin your hunting trip."

Outside it was raining hard. It is always raining when I go moose hunting.

We had planned a great trip. Just the two of us and the required guide in two canoes with minimal gear. We would strike out for the back country, portage the canoes into small, remote watersheds where we could hunt moose the old-fashioned way, beyond the reach of motorboats and floatplanes.

At dawn we loaded the canoes, two trim 18-foot wood and canvas beauties that smacked of tradition.

Soon Marcel showed up.

He was a short fellow wearing enormous unlaced leather boots, green pants, a red and black plaid shirt, and one of those unique little olive-colored, short-brimmed French Canadian hunting hats. He was sucking a toothpick and looking utterly destroyed.

"Too small," he complained, indicating the canoes with a jut of his chin.

"Plenty of room," I countered. "Two of us will travel in one canoe with all the food, clothing, and camping stuff; the other canoe is for moose meat, you, and your personal gear."

"There's no room for my personal gear," Marcel complained.

"All you need is your sleeping bag and a rain suit," I said. "We've brought all the rest. How much personal gear do you have?"

With that Marcel turned, sweeping his arm as if he were indicating the entrance of royalty, and gestured toward an immense heap of goods, most prominent among which was the mattress off his double bed at home, rolled and tied with a rope. There was also a 50-pound sack of potatoes, and a great carton containing 24 loaves of bread, plus an assortment of large plastic garbage bags stuffed with blankets, pillows, and clothes.

"When I go in the bush, I go comfortable," he declared.

As a result, we had to hire a motorboat to transport Marcel and all his gear. That meant we could only go where other motorboats could go, so we never did reach the silent wilderness we sought, and we never saw a moose either, except for one poor young bull that came out on a lakeshore one morning and was slain in a fusillade of shots from two motorboats full of over-equipped artillerymen that immediately converged on him with all guns firing.

The next year, when the mists curled like smoke over the water, and the frostbitten poplar leaves turned yellow and pungent, I again pursued my dream of a remote moose hunt conducted by canoe far beyond the throng.

My partner on this trip was Jim Henry, a two-time national white-water canoe racing champion and founder of Mad River Canoe Company. He had paddled this northern Ontario river the previous summer and had seen nine bull moose during the trip. He wanted to go back and hunt there and was looking for a partner. I signed on in a hurry.

To reach the northern zone, where the moose season opened in late September, we had to paddle through 40 miles of whitewater and make a six-mile portage around Thunder House Falls—we figured that would keep other people out. After killing our moose we would paddle another 100 miles north to a railroad trestle where we could flag down the Polar Bear Express freight train on its way to or from the arctic tidewater community of Moosonee on James Bay. We'd load the canoe, dead moose, and all our gear into a boxcar at the trestle and eventually wind up back in Cochrane, where we would leave a truck.

To provide an extra canoe to carry all the meat, we brought along a non-hunting paddler, Stan, who agreed to cook, keep the campfire going, and do camp chores while we hunted, for the chance to go along on the trip.

Now, this was a trip!

We ran the 40 miles of whitewater without difficulty and found that water conditions allowed us to shorten the six-mile portage to three miles. The pike fishing was good, so we ate well. It was raining lightly when we reached the northern hunting zone and set up camp the evening of the second day. By the following afternoon, the rain had turned to snow.

Despite the weather, there was moose sign everywhere, and we made strenuous attempts at calling with our birchbark horns.

"Sounds more like a pig," Jim said when I demonstrated my technique.

Nevertheless, late that afternoon, as snow fell steadily, a good bull came out of the forest across the river from my calling station, and I held behind the shoulder and fired three 30/06 rounds at a range of about 200 yards and heard the bullets strike. The moose crashed away, back into the forest.

I ran a mile upriver to where I had left my canoe and crossed the river, but by then it was dark and the search for my moose had to be delayed until morning.

We were back at the shooting site shortly after daylight. Finding the dead moose at the end of a half-mile blood trail was easy; the work began when we started moving it to the waiting canoes.

A large Canadian bull moose weighs about 1,400 pounds. The wet hide alone weighs 100 pounds; the antler rack about 75. Field dressed, the carcass may be reduced to half a ton of meat, bone, hide, and antler that must be cut into manageable pieces and backpacked to the river's edge.

By the time we had the moose loaded in the three canoes, moose hunting had lost a lot of its romantic allure. The 100-mile paddle to the railroad trestle still loomed ahead of us and the strong north wind would be spitting snow in our faces and slowing our progress all the way. We elected to split the moose we had, forget about going after a second one, and get the hell out.

It was a long paddle, but we reached the trestle in three days and arrived several hours before the southbound train was due.

There was a motley collection of shacks near the trestle. We had been forewarned that, while the inhabitants were normally honest people, they considered moose meat a commodity to be gathered by any means available whenever the opportunity presented itself.

"Don't leave the meat unattended," we had been advised.

So we took turns. One man stayed at the river with the canoes, one man portaged meat and gear, and the third stayed with the growing pile next to the railroad track.

It was my turn at the meat pile when the first Indian appeared, coming up the track with a wheelbarrow. A minute later another Indian stepped out of a shanty, dumped the trash out of his wheelbarrow, and began pushing it up to the track. Soon there were half a dozen Indians with wheelbarrows headed my way.

"What the hell am I going to do?" I wondered. I made a big display of pulling the 30/06 up across my lap and checking the magazine. The Indians seemed not to notice. They kept wheelbarrowing toward me.

The Indians stopped about 30 yards away and lighted cigarettes, eying me and my meat pile. I nodded at them and smiled, but they just glanced at each other furtively and said nothing.

"A standoff," I thought, trying to look tough.

Then Jim came up with the next load of meat. I tossed my head toward the Indians and gave Jim a raised-eyebrows expression of concern. He took in the situation; then, as if we were just two of a large party of hunters, Jim hollered down to Stan, "One of you guys bring the canoes up here—the rest of you stay down there unless we call you."

One by one, Stan brought up the canoes. The Indians watched, smoking, saying nothing, and making no moves.

Finally, the train came. When it pulled to a stop, a boxcar door slid open, and the conductor started throwing out packages that the Indians caught and loaded into their wheelbarrows, then trundled away.

"Hell," Stan said. "They weren't here for our moose meat, they were just getting their mail."

In retrospect, that trip stood out as a shining time so, two years later, Jim and I decided to do it again, only this time we would fly in with the canoes and skip the 40 miles of whitewater and the Thunder House Falls portage.

"Let's do it with muzzleloaders," I said.

"Sounds like a plan," Jim agreed.

We made up a party of four hunters; Jim, me, and our buddies Dean and Dave, and used two large canoes. We camped in the same place we had used before. It was raining, but there was lots of moose sign, and our spirits were high.

On the third afternoon, I called in a big bull.

It came out of the woods grunting loudly, just upstream from where Jim was sitting out of the rain under an overhanging bank. Each time I called like a lovesick cow moose, the bull grunted, then took a few steps closer. Soon it was no more than 35 yards from where Jim was sitting.

It was not until then that I looked at Jim. He was sitting there under the overhanging bank opening a candy bar. His position was next to a noisy rapids that blotted out all other sounds. He hadn't heard a thing. He hadn't heard my calls, hadn't heard the bull's answers, and was totally oblivious to the bull's approach.

I raised my birchbark moose call, grunted through it a couple of times for the moose's benefit; then, using the birchbark horn as a megaphone, I shouted, "Jim. Look up the riverrrr!"

He heard that. I saw Jim peek out from under the overhang. The moose was no more than 30 yards from him now and had come down off the riverbank and was walking closer through the shallows.

I saw Jim drop the candy bar and push back his hat, saw him haul back the hammer of his percussion lock, and watched him ease forward, raise the rifle, and fire.

The moose disappeared in the resulting cloud of white smoke, but was next seen walking slowly back up the river and around the bend, apparently unhurt.

"He missed!" I swore. "Big as a barn and not 30 yards away, and he missed!"

Jim dragged his canoe into the water and began humping the paddle, driving the canoe up through the rapids, following the moose. I jumped in the second canoe and followed.

When I cleared the rapids and paddled up around the river bend, the scene I encountered stopped me cold.

There was the moose, standing on the high bank. Its head was hanging down and blood was gushing from its mouth and nose. In his canoe, Jim was struggling to reload his muzzleloading rifle. I could see him dumping powder down the barrel, fumbling for a maxi-ball and finally driving it home, then searching for a percussion cap. Finally, he got the rifle loaded. He paddled closer to the moose, then raised the rifle and fired again.

This time the bull went down. It thudded on the high bank, rolled over, and fell into the swirling black depths of a deep river pool, then sank.

Now Jim was trying to reload again and, at the same time, paddling occasionally to keep his canoe from being swept back downstream into the rapids. I paddled up beside him, then we both paddled closer to the spot where the moose had sunk.

It was drifting just below the surface, and now and then an antler would swish up from below, then a foot would slice the water. I quickly rigged a loop in the canoe's anchor line, and the next time a hoof appeared I lassoed it and pulled the rope tight.

"Now you've got him," Jim yelled. "If he comes back to life he's going to drag you and that canoe off through the woods."

But the moose was dead. Jim's first shot had pierced its lungs and the second had brained it. Now the work began. Pulling as hard as we could the two of us were only able to draw the carcass into the shallows. There was no way would we be able to drag it ashore.

Though it was now snowing hard, our only course was to wade over our boots into the icy water and begin taking the moose apart. We hacked off a forequarter and hauled it ashore. Next we removed the other shoulder and pulled that up into the snow. With each removal, we lightened the carcass enough to drag what remained a bit farther ashore. Eventually we were able to cut off the hindquarters. Then the head and rib cage came ashore easily.

At dark we loaded all the meat in the two canoes and, though soaking wet and very cold, we paddled through falling snow and made it back to camp without having a wreck.

That night the campfire roared and the rum bottle went round and round.

We made a leisurely trip of the 100 miles to the railroad trestle and reached it with time to spare before the train came. This time the Indians with their wheelbarrows didn't worry us. When the train arrived traveling north toward James Bay instead of south toward our truck, we just loaded everything into boxcar number 1206 and looked forward to a night up in Moosonee.

But when the conductor came to sell us tickets he said, "Every Indian on this train knows there's a moose in boxcar 1206. If you don't want to lose your meat, one of you will have to stay in the boxcar tonight and nail the door shut from the inside."

We drew straws and Dean drew the short one. When we got to Moosonee we bought poor old Dean a six-pack of Molson Export and a couple of greasy cheeseburgers; handed him a hammer, some 2 × 4s, and a handful of 12-penny spikes; and boosted him into the boxcar with the dead moose, the canoes, and the gear.

Then the rest of us went up to the Polar Bear Hotel, showered up, ate steaks in the dining room, and later sent out for a bottle of Scotch that was delivered by a bootlegging Indian who scaled the hotel wall and handed us the bottle through our upstairs bedroom window, the hotel door being locked against such nighttime carryings-on.

Next morning we went out to the railroad yard and found our boxcar with Dean still nailed inside with the moose. I started whacking the side of the boxcar with a rock and Dean hollered from the inside, "What do you want?"

"Conductor says we gotta nail the door shut from this side, too," Jim shouted. "You've gotta stay in there all the way home. . . ."

Moose hunting is a funny business. When a moose trip is over you heave a great sigh of relief, and all you can remember is the hard work, the cold, the wet camps, and the incessant rain. I've never come off a moose hunt yet without swearing off moose hunting forever.

But the next autumn you start to recall funny stuff that happened. You hear the loons and the geese flying high overhead and smell the autumn leaves, and it reminds you of moose hunting, and before long you've got the maps out and are down on the floor running your finger over watercourses, noting the spots where you have seen moose or bet you could find one.

You pick up the phone and call your hunting partner and say, "I've been kind of thinking about another moose hunt."

And, if he is half the man he ought to be, he'll jump at it, "Me, too," he'll say. "Let's make a plan."

22

A WORD ABOUT MOOSE

The largest-antlered animal on earth is increasing in number and expanding its range throughout our northern forest states. The moose, mighty symbol of deep, remote wilderness forests, pristine lakes, and impassable swamps, is increasing steadily in intensely exploited commercial forests from Maine to Washington and down the Rocky Mountain chain into Colorado and Utah.

In fact, it is the commercial use of the forest that is driving the moose population to new highs, particularly in the Northeast.

Moose are creatures that thrive on forest catastrophes. Historically, forest fires, hurricanes and ice storms destroyed great sections of mature standing timber and created opportunities for new growth. Long-legged moose moved into these areas of mass destruction and strode over the broken stumps, tangled snags, and upended roots to browse on the succulent sprouts that emerged there. Today, the extent of such natural forest catastrophes is dwarfed by modern timber-harvesting techniques which create vast clear-cuts that quickly sprout up and become enormous reserves of new growth, ideal habitat for moose.

In Maine, which has more moose than any state but Alaska, moose numbers have been growing steadily from 20,000 in 1980 to more than 30,000 today, despite annual hunting seasons which now remove six to seven percent of the total number. In 1998, 2,000 hunters who drew moose permits in a Maine lottery harvested 1,840 moose, once again achieving a typical, yet astonishingly high, hunter-success rate of 92 percent.

According to moose biologist Karen Morris, the state's moose population could double in the years ahead if forest harvesting continues at current rates.

As moose numbers continue to grow at a rate of one to two percent a year, the moose population is spilling out of historic moose habitat and moving into smaller woodlands in inhabited areas.

Moose are very adaptable to living near people. It has become common for moose to wander down the main streets of country villages, crossing bridges, tangling clotheslines and garden fences, and drawing crowds of spectators. In Vermont, a bull moose recently declared himself the protector of a herd of cows and refused to leave them, eventually necessitating his destruction by authorities.

As moose numbers grow, moose-car collisions are increasing at an alarming rate. In a recent year, more than 700 moose were killed by vehicles in Maine alone. Five people lost their lives in those collisions, and many more were seriously injured.

Because of their great size (mature bulls sometimes weigh more than 1,400 pounds), moose generally stand their ground to defend themselves when attacked. Consequently, when the perceived "attacker" is a vehicle or train, moose are likely to stop and brace themselves rather than leaping out of the way. Because they are so tall (a bull stands 10 feet from hooves to antler tops), their eyes are above the level of headlight beams and reflect little light. To make matters worse, because moose are black, they absorb light. Vehicle headlights do not illuminate their bodies clearly, making them very hard to see on dark and misty nights.

Moose are relative newcomers in many parts of their present range. They moved south to occupy the Rocky Mountains only about 150 years ago and are continuing to spread into new territory. Only recently, moose pushed east and established themselves in Labrador. They did not exist in moose-rich Newfoundland until a small number were introduced there in the 1950s.

It is estimated that about one million moose now inhabit North America.

The moose range of North America is limited on the south by climate, as the animals do not thrive where mean summer temperatures exceed 60 degrees. They range north to the treeline where food and cover dwindle and barren tundra takes over.

Until about 100 years ago, moose and deer ranges rarely overlapped. Then land clearing and logging operations in the northwoods permitted deer to expand their range northward into moose range. And as the northern deer population increased, moose numbers began to decline noticeably.

It was discovered that the moose population was being harmed by accidental ingestion of infected terrestrial gastropods which are carried and passed by deer. This parasite rarely affects deer but commonly develops into a meningeal brain worm that can kill moose. In the 1950s and 60s, it was common to see moose in dazed condition, walking in circles and eventually dying from the effects of brain worm infestation.

Then modern clear-cutting practices came to the northwoods, and moose populations began to increase because of the abundant browsing opportunities provided by clear-cuts. Moose pushed south once more, moving into ranges that had been taken over by deer. As moose continued to increase and overlap with deer range, the brain worm problem began to have less effect.

It is possible that moose are developing a resistance to the parasite, but biologists think it is more likely that deer and moose are merely choosing separate feeding areas even though they occupy the same general ranges.

This could be happening because the clear-cutting, which is creating new moose habitat every day, is not conducive to heavy deer use. Deer feed around the edges of clear-cuts more than out in the middle. In winter, deer avoid exposure to cold wind and stay in protected places, while large-bodied moose just turn their rumps to the wind and continue to feed in the open despite the exposure.

Because moose are very impressive "watchable wildlife," thereby contributing heavily to northwoods tourism coffers, moose populations are being permitted to grow in all moose states right now, although the numbers of hunting permits issued each year is also rising in keeping with the population increases.

Right now, even though their permits entitle them to take animals of either sex, most moose hunters select for antlered bulls, which does not slow the population growth. Before moose in certain densely-populated regions reach numbers that cause unacceptably high vehicle collision rates or other unwelcome costs, moose managers can reduce the population and stabilize it at a justifiable number simply by issuing permits allowing a certain number of hunters to take females only.

Right now, and for the foreseeable future, moose in the Lower 48 have never had it so good, and excellent moose hunting opportunities will continue to increase.

23

FRANK RABBIT— LEGENDARY HUNTER

Old Frank Rabbit was an Ojibway Indian with a reputation as an exceptional moose caller. People said he was so good he could actually tell the moose jokes through his birchbark horn and kid them about their girlfriends' looks when he felt like being funny.

When I met Frank he was 75 years old, and as proud of the tally of children he had sired as he was of the number of moose he had slain during a lifetime spent in the bush. In the villages many women proudly declared Old Frank the father of this child or that one and smiled with the secret knowledge women have about such matters.

Frank himself carried the blood of a Scottish Hudson Bay Company trading post manager he said his mother jumped the fence with back in the days when his people paddled many, many miles each spring to trade furs and revel in the joy of having survived the deadliness of one more winter.

I met Frank on a moose hunt up in the Quebec-Ontario border country, probably the most moose-rich region in all of Canada. Hans and I had traveled by canoe into the heart of the country, set up a tent camp on a lake beyond the reach of other hunters and were ready to watch Frank do his thing, cajoling with the moose.

"I tease the bulls," he said. "I ask them what good are great big horns if you can only make love one month out of the whole year. I tell them I have women whenever I want, and prettier than theirs. I make them so mad they come out to fight."

It was mid-afternoon and our camp was readied.

"When do we start?" I asked.

"When it is dark," Frank answered. "When the wind is still."

"We can't do that," I said. "White men can't shoot after dark. It's against the law. We have to do it in the daylight."

"Me, I have killed hundreds of moose in my life," Frank retorted. "Every one at night."

Great, I thought. We come all the way up here to see this exceptional moose caller and he turns out to be a poacher!

"We will stand right here in our camp and I will make the calls," Frank explained. "You will hear the moose splash into the lake and swim toward us. We will wait. When he comes out of the water, I shine a light in his eyes and you guys shoot him."

So we had a showdown. I said we had to hunt in daylight, and Frank refused. He said hunting in daylight made no sense.

Frank explained that I would have to go far from camp to kill a moose in daylight, and then it would be a lot of work bringing the meat back to camp. "I can make the moose swim right into camp and we can kill him here where it's nice and clean and we have things ready for butchering," he argued.

Frank had it figured perfectly by Indian logic, and I could think of no rebuttal in terms of sportsmanship or game laws that refuted his wisdom. Killing a moose was not sport, it was a challenge, and carrying the meat is terribly hard work. A man who could convince a moose to bring its own meat right into camp possessed moose lingo oratorical skills of exceptional value.

As for the edict banning night hunting, well, that is a white man's law which does not apply to Indians. "We don't need lawyers to tell us the best time for hunting," Frank scoffed.

The issue was unresolvable. We could not hunt at night and Frank would not hunt by day. Furthermore, he said that if we were so foolish as to insist on killing a moose far from camp, he was too old to join in the childish folly of dragging the meat back through bogs and swamps to the ideal killing place where he had chosen to pitch our camp.

So, the two of us wound up hunting without Frank. We portaged a canoe three miles over boggy trails to a string of little ponds where Frank said a big bull lived.

We made a few calls, then sat down to wait. It was raining and we sat on the bank of one of the ponds whittling forks. The idea was that the guy who whittled the best fork would get the most peaches when we opened the single can Frank had sent along with us for lunch.

Suddenly, I heard a slurp and looked up. A cow moose had come out of the forest and was now wading along the opposite shore. If we had known anything about moose, we would have waited, for it was the season of the rut and there was a good chance that a cow would be followed by a bull.

But we didn't think of that. We were each allowed a moose of either sex.

"We better shoot her," I said. "The way this trip is going, we may not see anything else."

My partner fired, and the cow fell into the pond. With her last breath she let out a long death moan. That was all it took.

A huge bull moose that we had not known was following heard the cow's moan and came galloping to the shore of the pond, crash-

ing through brush like a tank. He burst out into view and stood toss-
ing his head back and forth, trying to shake off a willow bush that
had tangled in his antlers. The bush covered his entire head, and he
could not see out from under it, but we could see his wide,
palmated antlers, and it was clear that he was the biggest moose either of us had ever seen.

Now I fired, and the moose went down. He fell into an old
beaver house at the edge of the pond, driving one three-foot antler
so deeply into the tangle of criss-crossed alder branches that
we could not free it. The entire carcass was anchored by that stuck
antler and we could not move it. We had to get into the waist-
deep water and cut away sections of manageable size. It took us
all afternoon to take the bull apart and pile the pieces along the
shore.

We dressed and quartered the cow moose by moonlight. It was
very late when we slogged back to camp, wet, tired, and cold, leaving the big hunks of moose meat to await our return next morning.

When we told Frank of our great success, he shrugged. "That's
the bull I would have called right here to camp," he said. "You have
made much work for yourselves."

It was still raining when we returned to the meat piles with
pack frames and began assessing what we had in store. The bull's
antlers alone weighed more than 75 pounds, the two wet hides more
than 100 pounds apiece. About a ton of meat remained.

We figured it at 23 pack loads weighing 100 pounds each, and
could not begin to estimate how long each six-mile round trip
would take.

Frank's advice rang in our ears.

"You should hang the meat in trees and move your camp to that
place and stay all winter eating," he had said, and we knew that he was
right and that it had been imprudent to kill moose so far from camp.

We looked at the meat piles and then at each other and shook
our heads in dismay.

"If I live through this, I'm never going moose hunting again," my partner declared.

Just then we heard the roar of an approaching engine, and a moment later a little red floatplane appeared over the trees. The pilot spotted our meat piles and banked the plane into a steep circle. Then the plane landed in a rush of spray, taxied to shore, and a Quebec Game Warden jumped out on the pontoon.

"How many mooz' you got here?" he demanded in a thick French Canadian accent. Then he counted the scattered hooves and divided by four to satisfy himself that our claim of two moose really did account for all the piles of meat.

He checked our licenses, then glowered at us.

"You got two mooz' but only licenses for rabbits," he announced.

Petit gibier, I have remembered ever since, is French for Small Game, and that is what it said in big red letters right across the tops of our licenses. That we had paid for moose licenses but had been issued small game licenses accidentally, was a mistake that could not be satisfactorily explained while standing in the rain amidst heaps of moose meat on a lake many miles from the nearest telephone.

"I confiscate," the warden declared.

We helped him load as much meat as the plane could carry. It took about a third of the total.

"I fly this to *le bureau*, then come back for more," the warden said. "You stay here. Don't move any meat."

Hours later the little plane returned for a second load of meat. The warden had tried to check our claim that we had paid for moose licenses, but the investigation had been slowed because it was a Sunday, and he had not received an answer.

"I take another load; come back tomorrow for the rest," he said.

Thus the second third of our immense burden of meat was transferred without effort from our remote lake to a cooler at Fish and Game headquarters, and we trotted back over the trail to camp chuckling all the way under empty pack frames, having been ordered not to move the rest of the meat until our legal position had been determined.

When we told the story to Old Frank, he was chagrined at the manner in which we had been relieved of our responsibility to the meat pile.

He was even less impressed when our arresting officer flew in and landed at our campsite the next morning, returning our rifles and delivering a pair of big game licenses and moose tags along with his department's apologies for the error. As recompense for our "inconvenience," he offered to airlift the last load of meat to our lakeside camp.

"Now you will never learn why it's better to kill moose at night when you can make the moose bring his meat to camp himself," Old Frank grumbled.

He saw the whole episode as one more example of the white man's ridiculous need to complicate things. Airplanes, telephones, radios, offices, people filing papers, wardens flying around in the sky at great expense—all to perpetuate a system that allows killing moose irresponsibly far back in the bush, but taboos killing them at night when the moose would deliver itself to your door.

Afterward, I felt badly. I liked Old Frank and sympathized with his logic. By refusing to hunt with him at night, I had denied him an opportunity to display the skill on which his pride was hung, and by killing two moose without him, I was afraid it would appear that we considered his skill to be of insignificant value.

Thankfully, Frank didn't see it that way. His self-confidence was unshakable. He accepted the whole affair as another instance of absurd white man ways, and made it clear that he was different; superior was understood.

We offered Old Frank his choice of meat, expecting him to take at least a hindquarter, but he surprised us by saying all he wanted was the noses of the two moose.

"I know a woman who likes moose nose even better than beaver tail," he said with twinkling eyes.

That evening Frank deftly skinned out the moose noses and spread the meat to dry on a granite slab. Then he took the wet skin of the bull's nose and pulled it over his head so that his ears stuck out through the nostrils and the flaps made a short brim above his eyes and a longer one over the back of his neck.

"Now I have a good hat for rain," he said, grinning at us in savage splendor.

Each night we implored Old Frank to sleep in the tent with us, but he always refused, saying he preferred to sleep outside in the fresh air. Despite frequent rain showers Old Frank lay outside wrapped in an inferior sleeping bag under a canvas tarpaulin. If it rained hard he would pull his packsack over his head to keep the rain out of his ears and immediately go back to sleep.

"Me, I'm like a duck," he professed. "I only get wet to the skin."

In the morning he would be up before daylight, and we would arise to find him standing in a cloud of steam drying himself before a roaring fire. I asked him how he explained his vigorous good health, and he responded earnestly.

"I always swallers my food in chunks," he said. "Some people chew and chew their food until it makes a cement and plugs them up inside. I just bite my meat one time and then swaller it down. That gives your stomach some work to do so it doesn't get lazy."

Frank said that at 75, he was better with women than ever. "Until I was about 65 sometimes I was too fast," he confided. "Now that I'm older, I can take as long as I please."

We remained in the lake camp for several days, tending the meat under Frank's supervision and eating gargantuan meals of moose liver with onions and biscuits that Frank made in a cast-iron Dutch Oven set beside a driftwood fire.

Have you seen a moose liver? It weighs about 25 pounds and is purple and slippery. Frank kept ours hung in a tree. He broke off a dry overhead spruce branch and sharpened the remaining stub to a point.

Whenever he finished slicing what he needed for the next meal, Frank would carry the big, floppy liver over to the tree, lift the purple entity over his head, and slam it against the sharpened stub with a loud *fwop*. It would hang there in the shade all day, but at night a raccoon would come and pull the thing down, have a midnight snack, and leave the liver in a puddle just outside our tent where someone invariably stepped on it barefooted when going outside in the dark.

Frank found nothing peculiar about this.

Each morning he would exhume the bedraggled hunk of meat from the mud puddle, wash it clean in the lake, and start slicing off pieces for breakfast.

"The liver is the only part of a moose you should eat fresh," he told us. "The other meat would be tough if we ate it so soon."

All this happened more than 20 years ago, and I have never seen Frank since. But last summer I was up in Frank's country again and I inquired about him.

"Oh yes, Frank's still alive," a young Ojibway told me. "He's almost 100 years old, and just last winter he moved in with a new woman up on Wolf Lake.

"He's got so he thinks every good hunter is his son," the young Indian continued. "Mebbe you're my son," Frank says to them. "Tell me who your mother is. He always used to bring the women moose noses."

"What did they want with those moose noses, anyway," I asked my young informant.

"Oh, they didn't want the moose noses," he said, laughing. "What they really wanted was Frank."

24

CARIBOU HOUSE

Deep in the heart of the high mountain plateau that lies between Quebec's George River and the Labrador coast is a treeless escarpment strewn with boulders as big as houses. It is a land sprinkled with lakes that teem with trout and landlocked arctic char, a land cut by rivers where salmon thrive in unexploited abundance. Somewhere in that great expanse, according to stories handed down by many generations of Inuit, Naskapi, and Montagnais hunters, there is a mythical place from which all caribou spring forth. They call it Caribou House.

The exact location of Caribou House is now known, thanks to biologists who backtrailed the abundant herds to their ancient calving grounds. Caribou House exists right where legend said it was, comprising some 10,000 square miles of barren tundra where more than 160,000 new calves were born in 1987, bringing the number of animals now loosely referred to as the George River herd to more than 750,000 caribou. It is the mightiest caribou herd on earth.

The number is especially staggering when you consider that only fours years before, the George River herd numbered around 400,000 and that 10 years earlier than that a herd estimate of 125,000 was considered bountiful.

The caribou population of northern Quebec is expanding at a rate that is difficult to comprehend. The enormous George River herd gets most of the official attention because it is the one most accessible to hunters, but there is also the lesser known Leaf River herd that has surpassed the 100,000 mark and is continuing to expand at an estimated 13 percent per year. Besides that, there are obscure smaller herds on the Labrador peninsula, the north shore of the St. Lawrence River, and far south into areas where roads lead to the hydroelectric power projects east of James Bay.

When 10,000 to 12,000 caribou drowned in 1984, following heavy rains and an unfortunate dam release on the Caniapiskau River, the effect was barely noticeable, a drop in the bucket. Two years later sport hunters killed 8,593 caribou in northern Quebec and native hunters killed probably 6,000 more, but the total human harvest still represents less than one-quarter of the number by which the herd increased the year before.

Wolf predation on the George River herd, while increasing, is not seen as a major limiting force. The main reason wolves are not more of a threat has to do with the location of Caribou House and the migratory nature of the great herds.

At calving time, the George River herd marches north to Caribou House, where the barren habitat made up of lichen-covered rocks offers few wolf denning sites. The wolves den farther south in the taiga forest, where sandy eskers provide plenty of opportunities to dig well-drained dens. A heavy supply of hares, mice, and lemmings there provides a rich food source.

Thus, George River caribou calve in relative safety far from the country where wolves are raising and feeding their young. Wolf predation on George River caribou is unlikely until the calves have grown large enough to run and the great herds migrate south toward the better feeding grounds where the wolves are waiting.

Caribou herds that remain in the taiga forest to bear their calves are not expanding at anywhere near the rate at which the northern herds are increasing, and higher predation may be a significant factor in these slower growth rates.

Once the calves are born, the great herds disperse in all directions. Some herds drift off from Caribou House to the Labrador coast, others penetrate the valleys of the Torngat Mountains and press north all the way to Port Burwell. But the great mass of animals floods south from the calving grounds, crosses the George River, and spreads to the west. They fill up the valleys of the Whale River and the Tunulik, cross the Caniapiskau and the Koksoak, and spread out across the Ungava peninsula all the way to Hudson Bay.

During the hunting season in August and September, caribou move in a generally westerly direction, passing in vast numbers through regions where a number of native-owned sporting camps have been built to intercept the migration.

For many years, while the herds numbered far fewer animals, hunting camps along the George River were famous for hunter success rates that often hit 100 percent. But as the herds continued to increase, they began to eat themselves out of food. And as food resources along the ancient migration routes dwindled, the growing herds began altering their migratory courses, crossing the valley of the George River farther south and moving through areas that are accessible to the camps either at earlier dates or not at all. For a few years, the George River camps took a beating as hunter success rates dropped despite the fact that there were actually more caribou than ever. The animals were simply moving into new regions and migrating along new routes.

Caribou began showing up in great numbers in places where they had never been seen in living recollection. At Kuujjuaq (Ft. Chimo) thousands of caribou wintered within sight of the village and became hazards to airplanes landing at the jetport. Big herds began appearing up at Finger Lake where an Inuit man, Tommy Cain, operated a first-rate sport-fishing camp that was not then licensed to guide hunters. Fishermen at Finger Lake were casting for migrating arctic char while herds of thousands of caribou paraded unmolested in single file along the lakeshores. Today, the westward push of caribou continues all the way to Great Whale on the Hudson Bay coast and presses south to Chisisabi (Ft. George) in the Cree Indian lands east of James Bay. The herds now use almost all of the tundra regions of northern Quebec. Even the thin band of territory along the northern tip of the Ungava peninsula is now occupied in summer by the expanding Leaf River herd.

In 1984 the Quebec government began granting outfitters permits to set up temporary hunting camps in remote country near the new caribou migration routes. This move effectively put the George River caribou camps back in business.

Since 1984 the bag limit on caribou has been two per licensed hunter. Native tribal band members continue to hunt without limits, but electric walk-in freezers in the native villages have made it possible for them to keep their meat for longer periods, thereby lessening the number of caribou each family needs to kill.

It is the nature of caribou to be constantly on the move. They are here one day and gone the next, and as their numbers grow they must move even farther to find new grazing areas. The lichen called "caribou moss," which is the mainstay of the caribou diet, is a slow-growing plant that takes 50 years to regrow after being grazed off and trampled. If caribou stayed in one place and ate all the moss, they could not return in a man's lifetime. Instead, they keep moving, partially grazing the range in strips that parallel the paths they follow. At this time, there is not yet a food shortage, but recent caribou studies are showing early signs of stress from overpopulation. "The cows are calving a week to 10 days later in recent years," noted Quebec's wildlife management chief Gilles Harvey. "This means that they are ovulating later in the autumn, and we believe the delay is caused by the stress of migrating farther to find food—that and the nervous stress of overcrowding."

Despite the explosive growth of the caribou herds, most of the animals alive today will live more than five years and die of natural causes.

I have been traveling north to fish and hunt in caribou country for more than 30 years. Twice I have camped in the vicinity of Caribou House, and many times have visited other favored caribou haunts in the company of Inuit, Montagnais, and Cree hunters.

I recall a late September trip in the headwaters of the Ford River, a tributary of the George that flows out of the inner sanctum of Caribou House. I was staying with the Inuit hunter Noah Agnatuk and his family in their little tent camp on the shore of a very remote tundra-bound lake. I had been there several days but had seen no caribou. The migration had not yet reached Noah's lake. Then one night the hills around the lake echoed with the howls of wolves, and Noah came to my tent to tell me to listen.

"The wolves say the caribou come," he said.

Sure enough, the next day the hills streamed with migrating caribou. They came in long lines, one behind the other, an old cow leading each bunch and a bachelor band of bulls always bringing up the rear. For three days caribou passed everywhere, and then they disappeared as quickly as they had come. Next day, Noah and I climbed one of the higher hills and lay on our stomachs and glassed the distant tundra plains.

I looked and looked for caribou but saw none. I noticed that Noah was smiling, and when I asked if he could see "tuktu" he said yes and pointed far away. "Two looks away," he said to indicate the great distance. Still, I saw no caribou. I saw rocks, boulders of every size, and nothing of known size that could be used to gauge how big they were. When I finally picked out what Noah was looking at, I saw not caribou but a file of ants.

"Tuktu," he said. They must have been eight miles away, but they were heading toward us. Behind the first long line of animals came more and more.

Late that afternoon, when the migrating herd began trotting past us a quarter mile away, Noah stood up and walked toward them with his arms held high overhead like big antlers, and gestured for me to follow him doing the same thing. We walked with a swaying motion, trying to look like caribou ourselves. In that manner, we walked within close shooting range of the passing herd, drawing no more attention than a long stare from the passing animals.

Lines of cows with half-grown calves trotted past, their ankles making audible clicking sounds. Behind them followed groups of mature bulls with antlers so large they seem ludicrous.

I was shooting pictures when Noah pointed to a mountain pass where an enormously antlered bull caribou was trotting alone in the sunlight. His antlers soared out in a wide arc and were heavily furnished with broad shovels and long palmated tines. The rack surely exceeded six feet measured on the curve. (Racks measuring 84 inches have been recorded here, and average racks in that country measure four feet.)

"Good one!" I said to Noah.

"No good," he replied. "Smell bad." He was not impressed by antlers. Like all Inuit, he wanted tender meat, not a record rack from a bull in full rut.

On subsequent trips I hunted caribou at Weymouth Inlet on Ungava Bay, on the Korok River, on the George, on the DePas, the Leaf, and for several years on the Whale River where you can fish for Atlantic salmon and watch caribou cross the river while you cast. I hunted on the Finger River, the Gwenevieux, at Lac Dalhut, and far out on the 300-mile-wide breadth of tundra that separates Ungava and Hudson Bay.

For the first few years I shot for big racks and consequently wintered on tough meat, but I eventually outgrew that, and now I photograph the big bulls and only kill barren cows or yearling males for meat, the way the natives do. My whole family appreciates the difference.

Shortly after caribou started showing up regularly at Finger Lake, Tommy Cain, the Inuit camp owner, got himself licensed to take hunters as well as fishermen. In the years since, his camp has experienced impressive success.

Late one August I was there when the caribou descended from the east in streaming torrents that trickled over the barren hills and flooded the whole valley. Caribou passed between the buildings in the Finger Lake Camp and crossed the sandy beach where the canoes were pulled up. They flowed past the window in the dining cabin while hunters ate their breakfasts and were still marching past when the men regathered there for dinner.

How many?

"No man can tell," said Tommy. Until a few years ago caribou were rarely seen here, and then you saw only stray bands of four or five animals or the tracks of an old single bull. Now they come each year in ever-increasing hordes and, if you are there when a migration is passing, it is a sight that will live in your memory forever.

The caribou stayed at Finger Lake for three weeks that August. The herds moved along the lakeshores in a counterclockwise direction, traveling north on the east side of the lake and south along the west side. Thousands. Every hunter in camp filled out, and the natives from Leaf Bay settlement filled their big walk-in community freezer.

But the caribou left the night before I arrived early in September. That night they grazed off to the south and just kept on going. When I flew in I could see the fresh ruts where millions of hooves had rent the earth, leaving scars that would not heal in my lifetime. From the air I saw the white trails crossing shallow lakes that stood in the herd's paths, and I saw hillsides veined with an interwoven system of freshly used trails. But there were no caribou.

"Tuktu come back soon," Tommy Cain assured me as I got off the plane. "All gone now."

So for three days we traveled by canoe and climbed hills and looked around, and went back to camp empty-handed. That's the way caribou hunting is. Feast or famine. The Inuit know this and waste little time hunting for caribou. They just go to places where they know caribou will come, and they wait. While they are waiting, they make tea. They cook food over a fire. They fish a little. They search out protected places where they can get out of the constant wind, and sleep.

White men, on the other hand, scurry about in frantic efforts to find caribou where there aren't any. They wander far afield, walking back over the barren hills for miles and maybe finding a stray from a herd which, upon killing, they must drag back across the slippery tundra to the lakeshore. The Inuit smile at these antics. It's silly. There is no sense chasing caribou. When the time is right, they will come to you.

We waited at a crossing place where the lake narrowed between opposite points. When they returned, the caribou would cross at this place by the thousands. A person sitting still among the rocks could let caribou pass on both sides, not only seeing them up close, but hearing their ankle joints click, and the ruminating gurgles of their stomachs, and smelling the rich odor of the herd. There would be no sport in the killing, just clean, cool-headed shooting, each shot put straight through the lungs so the heart would continue to pump blood out of the tissues, making better meat.

When the shooting is over the Inuit draw their knives and begin skinning. They don't gut the animals, but rather remove the entire skin first and lay it flesh side up on the tundra. Then they separate the quarters from the carcass and pile them onto the clean skin. Legs are cut off at the knee joints. Backstraps and tenderloins are removed and piled on the skin. The neck is lopped off and thrown on the piled meat. The discarded rib cage is left intact, with the innards undisturbed until later, when the birds come along with the foxes and wolves. The whole operation takes but a few minutes; if the animal is shot correctly, the procedure is almost bloodless.

Several years earlier, my son Jeff and I had joined Tommy Cain and his son Moses and flown into the center of the Ungava peninsula to catch up with a herd that had passed Tommy's camp weeks earlier.

We landed on a little lake and made a tent camp so far beyond the treeline that we had nothing but willow twigs to burn and fires had to be limited to suppertime. There was not enough fuel to waste any for warmth. We cooked once a day and ate cold meat for breakfast and lunch. It was a chilling experience, but we had plenty of caribou meat and tea, and there were trout in the lake.

That time we shot eight caribou, and when we skinned and quartered them, Tommy and Moses piled the quarters inside the skins and tied them up into trunk-like bundles. They left the ears on the skin so that a leather thong tied around the neck skin would not slip off. Then we dragged the bundled meat over the snow-covered hills back to camp. When we came to a steep slope we sat on the meat bundles and rode them downhill like sleds, hooting and yelling like kids.

Now, I was hunting with Tommy again, but our sons had grown and moved on. Jeff was in Alaska learning commercial salmon fishing, and Moses had moved North and was hunting walrus.

"Good boys." Tommy said, nodding. "You, me, lucky."

We waited at the lake crossing and glassed the hills. Once Tommy saw a distant caribou, but it was alone and more than a mile from the lake. We saw a bear rummaging on the mountain slope opposite our spot and spent hours watching him.

This time our old friend Gery Emond of the Department of Indian Affairs was with us. He was building a burrow to get out of the wind. He excavated rocks with his hands and piled them up to make a blind complete with comfortable seats. He added a fireplace in one end while the rest of us gathered driftwood for fuel. By midday Gery had a good fire going and was boiling a pot of Labrador tea and broiling caribou steaks that Tommy had brought along with fresh bannock his wife had made in camp.

"No sense running all around," Gery said. "Until the caribou come, we'll make ourselves comfortable and wait."

From time to time boatloads of hunters would come by and stop for tea and a visit. At the insistence of their impatient white clients the Inuit guides were being pushed to burn excessive amounts of expensive gasoline running their outboard-powered freighter canoes up and down the lake looking for caribou.

"Caribou come today, Tommy?" the sports would ask as soon as their canoes hit the shore.

"Mebbe," Tommy would answer cheerfully. He didn't know and did not mind not knowing.

When pressed, he said he knew the caribou would return to this place because "they like it here."

He declared the caribou would come back three days after the wind changed. He explained that caribou like to graze with the wind in their faces. Since they had grazed south into the wind for three days, it would take three days of North wind to bring them back.

That afternoon the wind stopped. When it started again it was coming out of the north.

For two more days we waited at the lake crossing, eating caribou and bannock and swapping lies. The next day we traveled all the way to the south end of the lake and climbed a little hill. When the caribou returned they would show up here first, Tommy said. After that they would fill up the valley and be everyplace.

We had pulled the canoe ashore on a gravel beach at a narrow place where current from an incoming river flowed out into the lake. We could see schools of arctic char finning in the shallows in the clear water. They lay in the current in rows and swirled out of the way when the canoe passed over them. Char weighing more than 30 pounds have been caught here, and many of these fish appeared to be in at least the 20-pound class. Char season was closed, but I made a note to return here someday with a flyrod.

From the little hill we could see several miles up the valley. Ancient black spruce trees grew thickly in the lowlands, but the hills were barren, tundra-covered highland plains. The cold North wind blew steadily throughout the day. Late that afternoon the caribou returned.

An old cow led them, followed by a bunch of cows and calves, some yearling bucks, and barren females. I shot the two plump meat animals I wanted, and by the time we had them dressed and packed back to the canoe, more caribou were coming. We climbed the little hill once more and had a last look. For as far as we could see, caribou were streaming into view in lines that flowed down the hills and swarmed into the valley.

No one can tell how long the caribou abundance will last. Logic tells us that Nature will intervene and the great herds will die off so that the land can be rejuvenated and the cycle can begin again.

There are more opportunities to hunt caribou today than ever before. Jet aircraft operate daily between Montreal and Kuujjuaq (Ft. Chimo) and Shefferville, and caribou country begins at the end of the runways. From there bush planes serve hunting camps in the middle of country used by the most gloriously antlered big game species in North America.

25

THE POWER OF SUGGESTION

A party of a dozen American hunters were sitting around the table in the cook tent at a caribou camp up in the Ungava region of northern Quebec. Outside the tent the heads, capes, and trophy antlers of the bulls they had killed were turned upside down in the snow.

One of the guides, a young man from Newfoundland, had been preparing the heads for the taxidermist, and as a first step he had removed the tongues from the caribou skulls and put them in a big pot and set them on the stove to boil.

Now he entered the cook tent, took the pot of boiled tongues off the stove, set it on the table, took out one of the unappealing-looking organs, peeled off its outer skin, and began eating it like a banana.

"Help yerselves," the guide proffered, pointing to the pot. "They're good."

The hunters watched him with disdain. They looked at the unsightly gray, curled organs in the pot and glanced at one another with queasy expressions.

Then one of the the hunters, trying to be a good sport, forked a tongue from the pot, put it on a plate, and used his Swiss Army knife to slice off just the tiniest smidgeon of meat.

He put it in his mouth, chewed very delicately for a moment, then smiled and said, "You know, that's not bad. In fact it's good. It almost tastes sweet. . . ."

"That's right, Doc," the Newfie guide chimed in as he grabbed another tongue from the pot and bit off a chunk. "We always says, the more a caribou licks under his tail, the sweeter its tongue gets. . . ."

26

DRIVE-IN CARIBOU HUNTING

S am Tapiatic, a leader of the James Bay Crees, pointed off across the snow-covered hills toward a sweeping bend of the broad LaForge River, a tributary of the LaGrande, about 100 miles east of the hydroelectric dam called LG4 far out in the taiga forest of sub-arctic Quebec.

"I camped with my mother and father on that river bend to hunt and trap in 1960," Sam said. "We had to travel upstream in a canoe for two months from our village on James Bay to reach that place. Now we can drive here in five or six hours. If my father could see us sitting here in a truck he would not believe it.

"This was all my family's hunting ground," Sam continued. "When I was young we came up the river every year late in the summer and hunted geese and fished until freeze-up. When the snow came we would pack our belongings on handmade toboggans and drag them over the land to those far hills, where we would trap all winter. In the spring we would canoe down the river 300 miles to the trading post at Fort George on James Bay to sell our furs and visit with friends. We would be gone each year for nine months on trips like that. There were no roads here then.

"There were very few caribou when I was a boy," Sam continued. "My grandmother remembers seeing caribou only twice when she was very young, but then they disappeared and didn't come back into this country until about twenty years ago. Now they come each winter in herds of thousands and thousands."

I considered the man who stood before me. Born in a tent on a trapline, raised by his parents to be a primitive hunter and trapper until he was 14, Sam was then shipped off to school as a participant in a government native education program. He emerged as one of the first college-educated members of his tribe and became one of the chief negotiators of the James Bay hydroelectric project that won more than $100 million for his people. Now Sam helps invest that money for the Crees. The Noochimi Hunting Camp where we were staying is one of those tribal investments.

"We have had to become modern very fast," Sam said. "But our people's greatest strength is still our ability to live off the land."

Next morning Jim Henry and I left the warmth and comfort of Noochimi Camp and drove east into the pale yellow sub-arctic dawn. In the truck ahead of ours, Sam and his friend Eddie Pashagumiskum (Rippling Water) towed a trailer with two snowmobiles and drag sleds.

For more than 100 miles we drove at 50 mph on a ribbon of glare ice that was too cold to be slippery. "You can steer all right at this speed, but don't slam on your brakes," Sam cautioned over the CB radio.

We were heading out to Eddie's trapping territory, where there was a cabin and a big canvas tepee for storing furs and equipment. Our hunt would be conducted on the territory where Eddie's family had hunted and trapped for generations.

Caribou tracks crossed the road at countless places, and you could see where they had been digging in the snow for lichens on the hillsides above the road.

"They feed on the steep slopes where they can push the snow away downhill from them," Eddie explained. "They dig with their front feet and push the snow away with their back feet. They eat the moss that grows down there."

From Eddie's camp we roared north on the snowmobiles, Indians driving, clients riding in big wooden boxes on the drag sleds. The Indians had lined the boxes with piles of caribou skins to soften our jouncing ride and to give us some protection from the spume of snow that came off the snowmobiles and blew back over us.

Jim and I wore heavy insulated boots, while Sam and Eddie wore heavy hand-knit wool socks inside duffel cloth liners. The traditional Cree smoke-tanned moose-hide moccasins with canvas tops that extended almost to their knees completed their footwear. On their hands they wore leather work gloves under wool-lined moose-hide gauntlets that extended almost to their elbows. Their bodies were covered with heavy handmade sweaters, topped by fur-trimmed, duffel-lined parkas.

This was in January and the cold was intense. The air stung. It was −28°F. Caribou tracks were everywhere. I peeked at them through a narrow slit between my parka hood and face flap as we trundled and bounced over the snow.

The big herds that had moved into this area a month earlier had dispersed into small bands that foraged separately among the countless tundra-covered hills and valleys. At any time we would be within a few miles of a small roaming herd, but we would have to find it.

Once Eddie stopped on a little hill to have a look around while we waited for Sam and Jim to catch up. Minutes passed and they did not show up.

"Maybe trouble," Eddie said.

He spun the snowmobile in a tight circle, and we went flying back the way we had come. Eddie drove fast, and I bounced around in the box on the drag sled.

We found Sam and Jim in a perilous situation. They had been crossing a lake, following our tracks, when the surface crust broke and their snowmobile had plunged into a layer of wet slush that lay beneath. The slush had formed from the weight of the deep snow pressing down on the ice. This had caused water to gush up through cracks and saturate the snow on top of the ice.

Jim, on snowshoes, was dragging the sled away from the half-submerged snowmobile while Sam, in his moccasins, was chopping down Christmas tree-sized spruce trees and dragging them out to the wreck. It was so cold that ice formed instantly when air and water met, and the snowmobile was in danger of freezing into the ice.

At first I gave their efforts little chance of success. Freeing the snowmobile without getting wet feet before the machine froze into the slush seemed impossible. But Sam and Eddie knew what to do. They calmly set to work making a bed of spruce on solid ice beside the hole. Then the four of us heaved the snowmobile up onto the dry bed. They started the machine, then tipped it on its side and revved it up, making the freezing slush fly from the track and dolly wheels. Moments later the sled was reattached and we were off as if nothing had happened.

"How did you keep your moccasins from getting wet?" I asked the Crees when we stopped to make a fire and have a cup of tea.

"We quickly jab our moccasins in the water, pull them out, and let ice freeze like a skin on the outside before it soaks into the leather. When they have a skin of ice on them, they are waterproof. Now we have to be careful not to warm them by this fire or they will thaw and get wet." Then Sam and Eddie used sticks to beat the skin of ice off their moccasins. In a few minutes, the ice was removed and the dry moccasins were exposed.

At 1 o'clock we spotted a herd of maybe 20 caribou resting and feeding on a hillside about a mile away.

Moving behind a hill, we drove the snowmobiles in a wide circle to get downwind of them. We parked the snowmobiles in the cover of a little patch of firs, then strapped on snowshoes, slung our rifles over our shoulders, and began our stalk. Sam and Jim went off in one direction while Eddie and I split off in a flanking maneuver. Quietly, we snowshoed toward the herd using the terrain and little veins of head-high spruce to hide our approach.

When you advance from downwind toward a herd of migratory caribou that probably have never encountered men before, the animals usually don't spook. When we broke out of the spruce and began approaching them across the open snow, they stood their ground and stared at us. Trying to look something like caribou ourselves, the four of us held our arms outstretched above our heads like antlers and walked with swaying motions, swinging our "racks" to and fro. At 100 yards the caribou watched us without alarm.

For the Crees, hunting is a meat-gathering activity, not sport. Respect is earned by the hunter who gets close to the animals without disturbing them and kills cleanly with a single, well-placed shot. The Crees take fat cows and young bulls, not old bulls with big antlers and tough meat. Jim and I had elected to do the same.

Sam and Eddie were pleased when Jim and I dropped two fat cows with two shots.

"Good for eating," they agreed.

By the time we had the animals field dressed, Sam had a fire going and a teapot filled with snow dangled on a green spruce stick above the blaze.

"It is important not to hurry when it's this cold," Sam said. "After killing it is time to drink some tea and eat some meat to make us warm and strong for the cold trip back."

We broiled the tenderloins and hearts of the two animals on pointed sticks and ate them bloody rare.

"Eat this with the meat for warmth," Sam said, handing us each a frozen lump of lard he had dug from his packsack.

"Our children are taught in school not to eat fat, but our parents always told us we had to eat fat when we are out in extreme cold to keep from freezing," Sam explained.

The sun was sinking below the horizon now, and we were many miles from where we had left the trucks. "Should we get going?" I asked.

"We'll wait for moonlight," Sam answered. "You can't see well enough with just the lights on the snowmobiles. When the moon rises we will be able to see the land and know where we are, and we can take shortcuts instead of following our winding track backward."

I will always remember that bumpy hours-long trip back to the trucks, riding under the shining moon and stars in a box with a dead caribou in the brittle cold. I was cold, but not terribly uncomfortable, for the tea and caribou meat and lard had warmed me from within, and the bed of caribou skins was deep and protective.

The next morning a steady wind drove the windchill factor to a shockingly low number. We wondered if the Indians would refuse to go out in such weather. But instead of staying home, Sam and Eddie chose this extremely cold day to bring their wives, Sarah and Mary Ann and Sam's little 7-year-old son, Steven, along with us.

"When it is so cold, we need women to help," Sam told us. "They will keep a fire going near where we will be hunting."

Halfway to Eddie's territory, Sam spotted fresh ptarmigan tracks and stopped his truck. He and little Steven stepped deftly into simple Cree snowshoe bindings (twisted moosehide thongs that grip the toe and wrap once around the ankle) and plodded off into the bitter cold and deep snow, Sam with a shotgun and Steven with his air rifle.

Steven followed one of the white birds as it scuttled off under the spruces and killed it with a head shot when it paused to look back. His father gathered several more with his shotgun. In a few minutes father and son returned happily carrying their birds.

We crowded into the boxes, and once again we snowmobiled for miles until we came to fresh caribou tracks. Then Sam and Eddie left the women and little Steven at the edge of a frozen lake where there was a grove of protective spruces, and we drove off to hunt. While we hunted the women and Steven would cut and gather spruce boughs to carpet the snow and build a wind baffle beside it. They would cut and stack a load of firewood, then build a fire and begin cooking hot food for us to eat when we returned.

We roared off over the hills, following the caribou tracks. On the backside of a low range of hills we struck the tracks of a second herd, and Sam and Eddie decided to split up and follow both groups. Sam and Jim took off to the north, and Eddie and I continued west. Soon Eddie left the tracks and drove his snowmobile to higher ground from which he wanted to glass the country ahead before entering it.

We saw no caribou and moved on, staying high so we could see the country around us. After another hour Eddie stopped and pointed. About two miles ahead of us was a band of 30 or 40 caribou, traveling in a single line, crossing between two hills. We could see the antlers on the bulls even at that distance.

Once again, we dropped down to lower ground, then sped over the snow in a wide circle that would eventually get us ahead of and downwind from the herd. Eddie eventually stopped in a thin patch of spruce, and we strapped on snowshoes.

We moved through the band of spruces until we broke out on the side facing the caribou's approach. They were coming straight toward us, still several hundred yards away. There were half a dozen bulls trailing the cows and calves that walked ahead. My eye settled on a prime 2-year-old bull with graceful antlers. I pointed him out to Eddie.

"That one good to eat?" I asked.

"Yes, good," he said.

We huddled in the snow, not moving, while the females and young animals moved past. Then, when the bulls came abreast of us, less than 100 yards away, I raised my rifle, centered the crosshairs behind the young bulls's shoulder, and dropped him in his tracks.

When we walked up to the dead animal, Eddie pulled some hairs from the bull's chest near its heart. He rubbed the hairs between his hands and mumbled some words in Cree, then tucked the hairs under the snow.

Then Eddie made a little fire, and we ate tea and bannock and lumps of lard. This time we did not broil any meat.

"We go back to where the women are and have a feast," he said smiling.

We got there after a fast, rough, hour-long ride, and we were stiff with cold and crusted with snow when we arrived.

"Come by the fire and get warm," the women invited.

Soon Sam and Jim came in dragging another nice, young bull.

"Come here," the women beckoned. "There is tea and ptarmigan and warm bannock and wild berry jam. We will take the best parts of the caribou and cook them for you."

The deep carpet of spruce boughs they had made kept our feet up out of the snow and the wind baffle they had erected reflected the heat of the fire. Skewered ptarmigan breasts sputtered over the fire, and as fast as we ate them, they were replaced with broiled caribou tenderloins and hearts.

"When the hunters return we always have good food waiting," Mary Ann explained. "We have to keep the hunters warm and strong."

While the sub-zero wind screamed across the hilltops, we were warm and comfortable by the fire in our protected hollow. Little Steven, oblivious to the cold in sealskin mittens, fur hat, and smoke-tanned moosehide moccasins, was chortling with laughter and sliding down the hill on a little toboggan his father had made for him from the curved trunk of a tamarack tree.

"This is the way we have always lived," Sam told us when we had finished eating and were warm again. "Our people's strength comes from the land. Now that there is a road here, we hope that hunters from the south will come and join us and see that our land is not a wasteland, as some people say, but a rich region where Cree people know how to live comfortably."

He took a piece of caribou heart and held it in his hand and stared into the fire for a minute, then tucked the piece of meat under the spruce boughs. I asked him to explain.

"When we take from the land, we always think about what the land has given us and put something back," he said. "It is our way."

27

CARIBOU—
A CHANGING
CHALLENGE

Rivers of caribou were flooding down the hills and streaming through our camp. We could hear their ankles clicking as they trotted past, and the air was rich with their aroma. They came in long lines of cows and calves and young bulls, followed by bands of older patriarchs with enormous antlers that soared above them and tossed from side to side as they paraded by. It took all day for the herd to pass.

"Lots of caribou now, but some day the wolf will take charge," declared the Inuit leader Tommy Cain, who stood beside me.

It seemed an odd thing to say. It was 1987 and every northern Quebec hunting camp was awash with caribou. Caribou hunting was like shooting fish in a barrel. Success was almost guaranteed.

But Tommy was looking farther ahead, to a time when over-grazing or disease or a repressive birth rate would cause caribou numbers to drop so low that wolves would be able to keep those that survived in check while the overgrazed tundra renewed itself. It would take 50 years before the slow-growing, nutrient-rich lichens would stand ankle deep once more. Not until then would the caribou begin to cycle upwards again.

Caribou hunting in northern Quebec still has the highest success rate of any big game hunt in North America, but it's no longer the sure bet it was in the 1980s and early 1990s when the population soared to more than one million animals. Back then huge herds annually swept through the zones that were accessible from established hunting camps. It was easy for hunters to fill their tags with trophy bulls, and hunter-success rates approaching 100 percent were expected.

Today it's different. There are fewer caribou and the herds have changed their migratory habits. In addition, there are many more outfitters elbowing for a piece of the action.

Every indicator suggests that Quebec caribou have now passed over their population peak and are sliding into a long-expected retraction phase in which more caribou die each year than are replaced by new recruits. Furthermore, the huge herds that blanketed the tundra through the 1980s and early 1990s appear to have broken up into many smaller herds that have scattered across the land seeking new grazing areas. They no longer adhere to traditional migration patterns.

"This isn't a game farm up here; there are no guarantees of where the caribou will be," notes veteran outfitter Jack Hume, who has operated one of the most successful caribou outfitting businesses in northern Quebec for 28 years. "Quebec caribou are free to wander wherever they want in this roadless region which is more than twice the size of Texas."

A changing climate has added to the unpredictability of caribou migrations. For the past three seasons uncommonly warm weather in August and September has delayed the migration to the traditional wintering grounds and caused caribou to remain farther north where they stop and linger on inaccessible high plateaus where breezes give relief from blackflies and mosquitoes.

Even more frustrating for outfitters is that many of the older trophy bulls, which traditionally followed herds of females, calves, and younger bulls, have been gathering in separate herds in recent years, and migrating through regions where there are few hunting camps.

Migrating herds act as magnets. When they pass through an area they attract the scattered local bunches and carry them along, leaving an empty land behind. As a result, hunting success has been spotty since 1996. Hunters in some camps see thousands of caribou while those in other camps may see few. Nobody knows for sure which camps will be "hot" next week or next year.

Hunters paying $3,000 to $4,000 for guided, fly-in caribou hunts expect to see caribou. When the animals don't show, some clients get upset, especially when they learn that hunters in other camps are seeing plenty. Outfitters have had to cancel bookings for lack of caribou in certain areas. Others offer large cash credits to clients who do not get shots.

Despite its growing feast-or-famine reputation, caribou hunting has become a $50 million a year business in Quebec. It is generally accepted that increasing the annual harvest is the most effective way to thin the caribou population and avoid the catastrophe that would occur if the number of animals exceeds the carrying capacity of the range. Consequently, the government has encouraged outfitters to invest in camps and planes and cash in on the caribou while they last.

The outfitters' response to the changing caribou migrations has been to change hunting strategies. They are building spare camps in widely scattered locations, hoping that if one of their camps doesn't have caribou, another will; then use floatplanes to shuttle hunters to the locations that are paying off.

"Too many hunters are impatient," says Jack Hume. "They expect to see a lot of caribou right away."

Their clients' insistence on guaranteed success has led some outfitters to resort to unethical and even illegal means to provide shooting opportunities.

At the airport in Shefferville, departure point for many bush-plane destinations, I met hunters last September who were furious about how their "guaranteed hunt" had been conducted.

"We were stuck in a dirty little shack where there weren't any caribou for four days," one hunter explained. "On the fifth day the outfitter came in with a floatplane and said he would fly us to a herd. After a few miles, he spotted a little bunch of five caribou cows and calves swimming across a lake. He landed and told us to shoot them. When we refused, he said, 'I only guaranteed a shot at caribou. If you don't want to shoot, that's up to you.' "

A luckier hunter from a camp that had killed the limit complained that pirating outfitters brought in daily planeloads of hunters to poach on his outfitter's exclusive licensed zone.

"They landed right in front of our camp, unloaded their hunters, killed their caribou, loaded up, and flew away," he reported.

"Twenty-five years ago there were only eight caribou outfitters in Quebec; now there are 80 operating hundreds of remote hunting camps," Jack Hume notes. "Most of them try to do a good job, but there are a few bad apples with powerful political connections who get away with murder.

"Beware of any outfitter who offers a guarantee," Jack advises. "There's no such thing as a guaranteed fair chase hunt."

Some Inuit leaders say there are too many caribou camps and that older caribou are learning to avoid the regions where they have been shot at regularly. They say that the herds of 7- and 8-year-old bulls with the biggest antlers have lived long enough to find safer grazing areas and migratory routes.

Among the enormous number of caribou that still roam the 400,000 square miles of tundra and taiga regions in Quebec, a mere 13 individuals are wearing radio collars that are monitored by satellite. (There used to be 50 radio-collared animals, but the monitoring project is underfunded, and by 1999 only 13 collars were still operating.)

Until a few years ago aerial photographs and pilot observations led Quebec's Department of Environment and Wildlife to estimate that each radio-collared caribou represented a herd of at least 10,000 animals. Recent aerial observations, however, have shown much smaller herds traveling with radio-collared individuals.

Regular satellite reports plot the movements of the radio-collared animals. The information is available to outfitters who use it to predict where herds are headed and move hunters to camps where action is expected.

Last September, when I was at Jack Hume's camp on the Caniapiscau River, a herd about 3,000 with lots of large bulls had just passed through. The hunters who were leaving camp as we arrived had loaded up with good bulls. Now pilots reported that the country 30 miles west of us was full of caribou, but they weren't moving.

"We need an east wind," camp manager Barry Maurice told us. "Caribou like to move with the wind in their faces. With the right wind, they could be here in a day."

So we waited. We didn't jump in a plane and fly to the herd. Instead, we took stands at traditional crossing places along the river and watched. Autumn was turning the willow leaves to gold, and vivid red cranberries carpeted the tundra. Eagles soared high overhead, and we saw ospreys catching trout in the shallows. We spied on black bears patrolling the sandbars, looking for caribou carcasses.

We heard wolves howl and one morning watched a pack of five pass along the opposite shore.

And there were caribou. They were not in the big herds we had hoped to see, but every hour or so a little bunch would drift out of the trees, cross the sandbars, and swim across the wide river. The hunters from our camp were placed in pairs a mile or two apart, so any caribou that crossed our stretch were seen by someone.

Mostly, we saw cows and calves and younger bulls, but every now and then a few bulls with impressive antlers would be trailing them. When a hunter glassed a caribou that satisfied him, he would slip inside the riverbank willows and try to move into position to intercept the animal when it came to our side of the river.

We put in a lot of hunting hours, but that's what we were there for. Our vigilance paid off. By the end of the week each of the hunters in our party had killed caribou. None of the racks made any trophy books, but they made good memories, and the antlers meant more because they did not come automatically.

"I don't want to just fly to a herd and fill tags," my hunting partner Glen Smith confided. "Waiting and watching and hoping is what hunting is all about. A trophy rack should be a bonus to a good hunting trip, not a guaranteed outcome."

28

PADDLING TO ROCKY MOUNTAIN ELK

In the half-light of dusk, when white mist begins to form steamy curtains over the river valley meadows, the bugle call of a bull elk up in the forest makes your skin crawl. It is the eeriest of sounds. Whistling, wheezing, screaming, the notes mount from a profundo bass through several upsurging breaks, to end with a long, drawn-out squeal that echoes beneath the high peaks where snowfields shine under the silvery light of a rising moon. It is a sound so totally captivating, so surprisingly demonic, that your eyes widen and your ears strain to hear every nuance of the ghoulish shriek. Little hairs stiffen on the back of your neck and you stand in wonder.

In October, when the aspen leaves yellow on the hillsides and the first snows of the season whiten the awesome peaks of the Wyoming Range, the elk begin their migration down out of the high country toward the protected valleys where wild grasses provide a meager winter diet.

The downward migration pauses in the foothills. The elk are within striking distance of the protected sanctuaries and winter refuges. If early storms persist and snow deepens in the lower mountains they will push on, but until winter is ready to pounce, the elk hold back, feeding and breeding in the alpine meadows among evergreen forests that grow densely on the northern faces of the hills.

Most elk hunters say you need a strong horse to get into the best elk country, but my friend Harry Baxter of Jackson, Wyoming disagrees. Harry uses a canoe, and paddles in to elk country that not even horseback hunters can reach.

Harry has been elk hunting by canoe ever since he moved to Wyoming from Maine. Five times winner of the National Whitewater Championship, Harry automatically thinks in terms of what he can do with a canoe. When he wanted to go elk hunting, he studied maps, looking for blocks of country cut off from roads by cliffs and canyons that could be reached by water. Harry paddles in, sets up a tent camp, and hunts the hills above the river. He kills an elk each year this way, and some of them have been enormous bulls that rank high in trophy measurements.

A highway that runs along the Snake River winds through some of the best elk country. Horseback and foot hunters alike park their rigs at certain places along the highway and travel back in to the hills to hunt. Harry parks in the same places, but he goes the other way.

Instead of climbing into the hills, Harry slides his canoe down over the bank, slips across the river to the side where there is no road, and immediately enters a peaceful chunk of country in which he will be the only hunter. The tent goes up, firewood is laid in, sleeping bag rolled out. In minutes, Harry's elk camp is complete, and for all the company he'll have he could be 50 miles back in the wilderness.

The weather is perfect for camping in Wyoming in October. Sunny days and frosty nights are the rule, and nothing sets you up for a better night's sleep than hiking in that steep country. You rise by starlight and by the time the first gray light begins to gather over the eastern mountains, you want to be a mile or so up in the hills, 1,000 feet or more above the riverside campsite.

The forest grows in patches: hillsides of aspen give way to spruce and lodgepole pine, but here and there among the trees you come upon natural glades and open grass meadows. Elk sign is everywhere. Trails are beaten into the dry earth, with heart-shaped cloven hoof prints vivid in the damper places. Droppings litter the ground in places where elk have bedded.

Occasionally you come across a young pine that has been ravaged by a bull elk; the branches are broken for six feet up from the ground, and the bark hangs in shreds. The aspens along heavily traveled elk trails are rubbed and gouged by antler points. And in wet areas you find the wallows: muddy, trampled places where big bulls tread their urine into the earth, marking their territories with stinking assertions of their lust.

The big bulls only bugle in areas where they feel safe. You rarely hear them in country that is easily accessible to hunters. But here, where they have not encountered people, the herd bulls send out their defiant challenges at dawn and dusk, shattering the silence of these lonely hills.

Hunting in such country on your own and on foot, without even the creaking of saddle leather and the snorting of horses to distract you from the natural sounds and smells, you can't help experiencing an elemental lift. Alone in this magnificent country with breathtaking views in every direction, you stand upon a mountaintop in the cool, thin air and are overwhelmed by a feeling of discovery and well-being. Elk hunting is like that when you get away from others and hunt in country that you can have to yourself.

You work up through the timber, alert to every sound and smell. Now and at dusk is when you may spot a band moving across an open place. A ruffed grouse bursting into flight jars you like a jolt of electricity.

In the timber, fresh sign slows your progress to a near standstill. The ragged lines of broken trees, upended roots, and fallen branches, together with the deep contrast between dark shadows and patches of sunlight, make it possible for elk to be close without being noticeable. You must stop and study every form. If you do come across elk in the thick growth, you are not likely to see a whole elk at once. You must search for something that doesn't quite fit, a piece of an elk.

Prowling through the timber, you begin to learn the territory. Following the elk trails, you find where tiny springs seep up from the arid soil and provide little pools of drinking water for elk that rarely come out into the open to drink during midday. At the wallows you learn to identify the distinct odor that some hunters can distinguish from a distance and know when elk are near.

Late in the morning, when your senses are dulled by too many hours of suspended anticipation, it's nice to climb to a promontory and eat your lunch in the sun and soak up the country that stretches out around you: endless steep mountainsides, peaks, and mountains shining with snow, the river a thin blue ribbon far below you now.

When Harry Baxter shot this year's elk, a 5-point bull, he was about three miles from where we had camped together and more than 1,000 feet above the river. Just before dark, heading back down to camp after a day-long hike that had taken us high into the mountains, Harry came to the edge of an alpine pocket where we had been seeing fresh elk sign for several days.

The sun was setting and the sky reflected a pinkish alpenglow. Harry wanted to be back in camp by dark, for the steep, jumbled hillside is no place to be walking without a light. He figured there was time to circle this last hillside, then drop down into the river valley and be coming home on the flat river trail when darkness overtook him.

Jim Henry and I reached camp just about dark and built a roaring campfire, poured cups of whiskey, and waited for Harry. An hour later we were still waiting.

"He won't be coming in now," Jim said. "Too dark."

If he'd been caught by darkness in the high country, Harry would spend the night where he was rather than risk breaking an ankle descending the mountain in darkness. We knew he carried a down vest, extra woolen socks, and an aluminum space blanket in his daypack. He'd build a little fire and spend the night where he was.

"I guess we can drink his ration of whiskey," Jim said, doling out an extra drink.

But before we sipped it, we heard a crack in the woods, and then Harry came looming into the firelight. Dried blood smeared his arms. He carried a bloody cheesecloth sack, and a tired grin split his tanned face.

"I thought we ought to have fried elk heart for dinner," he said, holding up the sack.

Harry had done it again. One more elk would go home in his canoe.

Slipping along the backside of the mountain at sunset, Harry had suddenly smelled elk. "The air was still, and I hit a wall of elk scent," he told us. "It was as distinct as if I'd just walked into a cow barn."

Harry had stopped and let his gaze slide over the woods. In a moment a cow elk appeared, followed by another. Then two more cows stepped out of the trees. A moment later Harry could count seven antlerless elk along the edge of the timber. His heart was pounding. There had to be a bull tending a bunch like this.

The last of the elk crossed the opening and disappeared into the forest. No bull had shown himself. Harry wondered if maybe the bull had crossed ahead of the cows. But he knew that bulls usually follow their harems, so he waited and watched the alpenglow getting dimmer.

Then, without a sound, the bull stepped out of the forest only 50 yards away.

"He had been standing there the whole time and I never saw him," Harry said. "If I had moved, he would have been out of there."

If there is anything better than sliced elk heart lightly salted and peppered and seared in a little butter in a black iron skillet over the coals of a cottonwood fire with the river muttering in the background, you'll have to tell me about it. No filet mignon was ever more tasty or tender.

When the moon crept up over the mountain that night, a great horned owl lit in the tree above our campfire and looked us over with shining yellow eyes. Back in the hills, coyotes were talking back and forth between mountainsides. It was one of those perfect moments at the end of a good hunt when it seems you are especially in tune with nature. You and the owls and the coyotes are one, predators all, exhilarated enough to think that a successful hunt and a full belly are worth hooting and howling about, yet absolutely satisfied with one good kill and in no rush to make another.

INDEX

Absaroka range, 131
aerial photos, to predict herd
    movement, 109, 201
Agnatuk, Noah, 177–78
airplane transportation, 49, 184,
    202–02
Alain (guide), 58, 61
Alberta Clipper, 144
antelope, 133, 136
Anticosti Island, 47–55
    accommodations, 48–49, 55, 58,
        88
    beaches, 58, 62
    calling deer on, 58–61, 88–99,
        101–06
    horseback, hunting on, 57–64
    peat bogs, 60, 62
    predators, lack of, 48, 63
    Riviere aux Plats camp, 58
    secrets of success, 48–49, 55,
        63–64
    transportation to, 49
Anticosti Outfitters, 88
antlers
    rattling, as call, 26, 58–59, 60–61,
        87–99, 113
    rubbing, 6, 109, 111, 113
Any-deer permits, 84–86

backtrails, 18–19, 66–67
Balch, Alfred, 13–21, 147–52
Baxter, Harry, 133–34, 136, 204–08
Bell River Lodge, 88, 102

Big Horn range, 131
Big Horn River, 137
birch bark calls, 148, 150, 155, 158,
    165–66
Blacksmith, Paul, 148
boats, hunting by. See canoe
    hunting
Brothers, Al, 119
bucks
    bedding places, 25
    determining age of, 84
    evasion tactics of, 18–19, 66–67
    fighting among, 26, 92–95
    hoof tapping by, 104–06
    old, 73, 95, 113
    territoriality, 26
    tracks of, 16–17, 58
    travel patterns, 21, 24–26, 73
    young, 84, 86, 114, 117–20
bucks, trophy
    behavior of, 112–14
    evasion tactics of, 6, 8–12, 27
    in Kenauk Reserve, 75–76
    in Montana, 143–46
    most memorable, 121–25
    selecting for, 83–86, 117–20
    tracking, 5–12, 20–21, 108–15
    travel patterns of, 6–7, 21, 26–27,
        50, 108–09, 111, 113
bugling, of elk, 205
bulls, trophy (caribou), 199–202
Bureau of Land Management
    (BLM), 137, 140

Cain, Tommy, 176, 179, 181–83, 197–98

calls, to attract deer
  doe bleat calls, 101–06
  grunt calls, 19, 60–61, 113, 115
  hoof tapping, 104–06
  rattling antlers, 26, 58–59, 60–61, 87–99, 113

calls, to attract moose
  birch bark, 148, 150, 155, 158, 165–66
  chainsaw, 148–49
  Maxwell House Moan, 149

Caniapiskau River, 174, 175, 201

canoe hunting
  for deer, 23–27, 37–46, 131–37, 139–46
  for elk, 204–05
  in freezing weather, 37–46
  for moose, 147–52

caribou
  collisions with vehicles, 176
  diseases of, 198
  feeding habits of, 176–77, 182–83, 189, 198, 201
  herd size, 198–99
  hunting regulations, 176
  migration of, 174–80, 182–83, 188–90, 197–201
  population size, 174–77, 188, 197–99
  presence revealed by birds, 20
  tongues of, 185–86

Caribou House, 173–84

caribou moss, 176–77

caribou outfitters, 198–201

chainsaws, to attract moose, 148–49

char, arctic, 183

Chicotte River, 58

Chisisabi (Ft. George), 176

clear-cutting, and herd size, 161–64

Cleary, Pat, 20

clothing for hunting, 67, 189, 190–91

counterfeit deer, 9

Cree Indians, 177, 187–95

crops, deer movement near, 109, 111, 114–15, 133, 140

decoys, 9

deer
  antler rubbing by, 6, 109, 111, 113
  bedding places, 11–12, 25, 66, 71–72, 113
  behavior of, 112–14
  breeding, 50, 88–89, 102
  death of, 118
  droppings, 16
  evasion tactics, 6, 30, 110–12
  feeding habits of, 24, 71
  fighting among bucks, 26, 92, 95
  habits, 14, 24–26
  management programs, 48, 63–64, 83–86, 117–20
  migration of, 40–41, 43, 49–50
  mule. *see* mule deer
  nutrition, 84–85
  response to rattling, 88–99
  rutting, 6, 16–17, 58, 92, 95
  scrapes of, 6, 11, 17, 26, 111, 113
  sex of, 16–17
  territoriality, 26
  whitetail. *see* whitetail deer

See also bucks; bucks, trophy;
  does
deer drives, 77–78
deer yards. *see* yarding areas
DePas River, 178
Devost, Rolie, 57–58
Diem, Al, 90
diseases
  of caribou, 198
  of moose, 163–64
does
  attracting, 92–93, 104–06
  bleat call, simulating, 101–06
  droppings of, 16
  following bucks, 20
  hiding from bucks, 50, 51, 53, 89
  migratory habits, 73
  permits to kill, 84–86, 118–20
  tracks of, 16
dogs, hunting with, 77–78
Dream Seasons, 108
dreams of deer, 12, 30–31
droppings, determining sex by, 16
Drury, Mark and Terry, 107–08
  observations on deer behavior,
    112–14
  tips for shooting trophy deer,
    114–15

elk, 133, 136
  bugling by, 205
  feeding habits of, 203–04
  migration of, 203–04
  scent of, 206
  wallows, 205, 206
Emond, Gery, 182

Field and Stream magazine, 1
Finger Lake, 176, 179
Finger River, 179
Ford River, 177

Gagnon, Jean, 101–03
Gagnon, Siegfried, 77–80
Galant, Normand, 49–55
game preserves
  Anticosti Island, 48
  harvest restraints on,
    119
  Kenauk Reserve, 75–81
  Port Cartier, 147–52
Gaspé peninsula, 47–48
George River caribou herd, 173–84
Georgia, deer management
    program, 120
Great Whale, 176
grunt calls, 19, 60–61, 115
guaranteed hunt, 200
guides, hunting with, 77–78, 153–54
Gwenevieux River, 179

Harvey, Gilles, 177
Henry, Jim, 31–34, 133, 154–60,
    188–95, 207
hoof tapping, by bucks, 104–06
horseback, hunting on, 57–64
Hume, Jack, 198, 200, 201
Hunter's Moon, 113
hunters, other
  avoiding, 23
  hunting pressure by, 25, 27, 154,
    198–201
  rattling antlers and, 98, 109
hunting

on Anticosti Island, 47–55, 57–64
for big bucks, 6–8, 10–12, 75–76,
    107–15
for caribou, 173–84, 187–95,
    197–202
clothing for, 67, 189, 190–91
as connection to ancestors, 2–3
with dogs, 77–78
for elk, 203–208
in freezing weather, 37–46,
    187–95
with guides, 77–78, 153–54
on horseback, 57–64
luck and, 29–35
in Montana, 139–46
for moose, 147–52, 161–64,
    165–72
by Native Americans, 2
at night, 166–68, 170
observation stands, 110–12, 115
with partners, 18–19, 67, 89–91
smoking, spitting, urinating
    while, 112
by snowmobile, 187–95
on snowshoes, 190–91, 194
for whitetail deer, 69–73, 140–41,
    146
in Wyoming, 131–37, 203–08
See also canoe hunting; scouting;
    stillhunting; tracking
hunting camps
    Anticosti Island, 47–55
    Noochimi, 188
    in Quebec, 197–201
    Riviere aux Plats, 58
hunting permits and licenses
    Any-deer, 84–86

for caribou, 176
as herd management tool, 83–86,
    117–20
in Montana, 140
for moose, 162, 164, 169–70
in Wyoming, 137
hunting zones
    on Anticosti Island, 50–52, 55,
        60–61, 89
    in Kenauk Reserve, 77

Indians
    Canadian, 20, 88, 147–52,
        156–57, 173–84
    Cree, 177
    Montagnais, 20, 147–50, 173,
        177
    Naskapi, 173
    Native Americans, 2
    Ojibway, 165–66
Inuit, 173, 176, 177, 179–82,
    200–201

James Bay, 187
Johnny Stewart, Inc., 89
Jupiter River, 49

Kenauk Reserve, 75–81
Kilgore, Rob, 122
Kilsoak River, 175
Knights, Roy, 75–76, 79–80
Korok River, 178
Kuujjuaq (Ft. Chimo), 176,
    184

Lac Dalhut, 179
Lac Pasteur, 149

LaForge River, 187
LaGrande River, 187
Lake Maholey, 79
Lavigne, Gerry, 71, 84, 86
Leaf Bay, 179
Leaf River, 176, 178
LeBrasseur, Normand, 88–91, 95
Levesque, Jean-Marc, 104–106
Lewis and Clark, 140
LG4 hydroelectric dam, 187
lichen, as caribou food, 176–77, 198
luck, hunting and, 29–35

Maine
    canoe hunting, 27
    deer management program,
        83–86
    deer migrations in, 70
    moose population, 162
maps, to predict deer movement,
    109
Marcel, guide, 153–54
Maxwell House Moan, 149
meat
    of caribou, 178, 179, 183,
        185–86, 194
    of deer, 52, 125, 134, 140
    handling carcass, 27, 60, 156,
        159, 168–70, 181
    stealing, 127–29, 155–56, 159–60
Menier, Henri, 48
Merlo, Tony, 80–81
Michigan, deer migrations in, 70
migration routes. *see* travel patterns
Minnesota
    canoe hunting in, 27, 37–46
    deer migrations in, 69–70

missed shots, 7–11, 35, 92–96
Missouri Breaks, 139
Missouri River, 139–40, 142
Monster Bucks, 108
Montagnais Indians, 20, 147–50,
    173, 177
Montana
    canoe hunting in, 27
    deer hunting in, 139–46
    deer migrations in, 70
Montibello, 75
moon, influence on deer, 113
moose
    calls to attract, 148–50, 155, 158,
        165–66
    collisions with vehicles, 162–63
    expanding range of, 161–64
    livers of, 171–72
    living near people, 162
    in northern Ontario, 153–60,
        165–72
    noses of, 170–72
    parasites of, 163–64
    in the Port Cartier Reserve,
        147–52
Moosonee, 155, 159–60
Morris, Karen, 162
movements
    of deer, 7, 11, 19
    of hunters, 15, 19–20, 65–67
mule deer
    in Montana, 140, 143–46
    in Wyoming, 131–37
muzzleloaders, 157

Naskapi Indians, 173
National Scenic River Act, 140

Native Americans, 2
New Hampshire
    canoe hunting in, 27
    deer migrations in, 70, 71–72
Noochimi Hunting Camp, 188
North Platte River, 137
Nowell, Bill, 77, 80

observation stands, 110–12, 115
Ojibway Indians, 165
Ontario
    deer hunting in, 27
    moose hunting in, 153–60, 165–72

packhorses, 59–60
partner hunting, 18–19, 67, 89–91
Pashagumiskum, Eddie (Rippling
        Water), 188–94
Pickett, Fred, 127–29
Polar Bear Express, 155, 159–60
Polar Bear Hotel, 160
Port Burwell, 175
Port Cartier Reserve, 147–52
Port Menier, 49
predators, 118
    on Anticosti Island, 48, 63
    of caribou, 174–75, 197–98
private land, 136, 140
Producing Quality Whitetails
        (Brothers and Murphy), 119
ptarmigan, 193–94
public land, 137, 140

Quality Deer Management
        Association (QDMA), 119–20

Quality Deer Management (QDM),
        119–20
*Quality Whitetails, The Why and
        How of Quality Deer
        Management* (Miller and
        Marchinton), 119–20
Quebec
    Anticosti Island, 47–55, 57–64,
        88–89
    canoe hunting in, 27
    caribou hunting in, 173–84, 187,
        197–202
    Department of Environment and
        Wildlife, 201
    Montibello, 75
    Port Cartier Reserve, 147–52
Quebec City, 49

Rabbit, Frank, 165–72
radios
    for communicating, 78, 140, 188
    to track herds, 201
railroad transportation, 155, 159–60
rattling antlers, 26, 58–59, 60–61,
        87–99
    in breeding season, 88
    difficulties of, 90–96
    before rutting season, 98, 113
    synthetic vs. real, 89, 98
    tips for using, 89–90, 98–99
rifles
    Remington, 80
    Ruger, 35
Riviere aux Plats camp, 58
rubs, of bucks, 6, 109, 111, 113

rutting, 6, 58
    deer calls and, 84, 89–90, 92
    tracks indicate, 16–17

Sapp, Werner, 81
scent, of hunters, 111, 112
scopes, Leopold, 52, 80
scouting, 108–09, 137
scrapes, used by deer, 6, 11, 17, 26,
    111
Sept Îles, 49
shadows, staying in, 19, 65–66
Shefferville, 184
shooting
    first deer, 14, 121–25, 127–29
    from horseback, 60
    missed shots, 7–11, 35, 92–96
    at night, 166–68, 170
    rattling antlers and, 89–97
    trophy deer, 114–15
Shoshone River, 137
shotguns, 123–25, 128
Snake River, 137, 204
snowmobiles, 187–95
snowshoes, 190–91, 194
sounds, 57–64
    bugling, of elk, 205
    made by deer, 19, 26
    made by dogs, 78
    made by hunters, 19–20, 66–67
    of other animals, 20
    See also calls, to attract deer
South Dakota, deer migrations in, 70
Southeastern U.S., deer migrations
    in, 70

Sports Afield magazine, 1
St. Onge, Bozo, Lucien, and
    Homer, 147–52
stillhunting, 13, 65–67
    on Anticosti Island, 63–64
    in Kenauk Reserve, 77–78
    in Wyoming, 134
summer ranges, of whitetail deer, 70

Tapiatic, Sam, 187–95
territoriality, 26
Terry, Bill, 134, 135
Thunder Horse Falls, 155, 157
tobacco, to lure moose, 147–52
Tomas Ranch, 89
Torngat Mountains, 175
tracking
    big bucks, 5–12, 20–21, 27,
      108–15
    determining sex of deer, 16–17
    elk, 205–06
    finding migratory trails, 72
    hunting parallel to track, 18–19,
      51, 66–67
    learning habits of deer, 14,
      24–26, 112–14
    movements of hunters, 15, 19–20,
      65–67
    near waterways, 24–27
    rain and, 17, 26, 109
    spotting deer, 15, 66
    weather conditions and, 17, 26,
      150–51
    See also stillhunting
tracks

of caribou, 189
determining sex by, 16–17, 58,
  147
determining size by, 108
direction of, 18, 21, 66
reading with fingers, 15–16
recognizing individual, 6–7,
  20–21
trapping, 187–89
travel patterns
  of big bucks, 6–7, 21, 26–27,
    109–11, 113
  caribou migration, 174–80,
    182–83, 188–90, 197–202
  influence of crops on, 109, 111,
    114–15, 133, 140
  near waterways, 23–24
  observing, 14, 26, 72–73, 108–09
  tracks indicating, 18, 21, 40–41,
    43, 66
  whitetail deer migration, 69–73
trophy deer. *see* bucks, trophy
Tunulik River, 175

Underwood, Lamar, 1
Ungava peninsula, 176, 178, 185
U.S. Forest Service, 137
U.S. Park Service, 137

venison. *see* meat
Vermont
  canoe hunting in, 27
  deer migrations in, 70

wallows, of elk, 205, 206
waterways, hunting near, 23–27. *See
  also* canoe hunting

weather conditions
  on Anticosti Island, 63–64
  and caribou migration, 182–83,
    201
  cold-weather hunting, 37–46
  and moose ranges, 163
  rain, 17, 26, 109
  tracking and, 17, 26, 150–51
Weymouth inlet, 178
Whale River, 175, 178–79
whitetail deer
  on Anticosti Island, 47–48, 55,
    57–64
  in Montana, 140, 141, 146
  selecting for big bucks, 117–20
  summer ranges of, 70
  in Texas, 89
  tips for hunting, 108–15
  winter migration of, 69–73
  winter ranges of, 70–71
Whitetail Madness, 108
wind, and caribou migration,
  182–83
Wind River, 137
winter ranges, 41, 70–71
Wisconsin
  canoe hunting in, 27
  deer hunting in, 30
wolves, 174–75, 177, 197–98, 202
Wyoming
  elk hunting in, 203–208
  mule deer hunting in, 131–37
Wyoming Range, 203

yarding areas, 6, 70–71